THE THOUGHTFUL DOG TRAINER

PRAISE FOR THE BOOK

As the title suggests this book is an exploration of the strengths and weaknesses of our own minds and is as much self-help guide as it is training manual. With disarming honesty, Jo uses her own experiences of managing ill health and dealing with tragedy to explore how we can build our own confidence and competence to provide a clear framework for our working dogs. It's an extensive deep dive into the mindset of owning and training a dog and includes some very helpful devices of the author's own creation to provide a fallback system for those looking for assistance. I don't want to say much more for fear of stealing her thunder but it's a refreshingly honest investigation into the entire hinterland of our relationship with dogs, including plenty of very helpful material to structure your training around. So, whether it's a self-help guide or a training manual, it's a fascinating read with plenty of practical assistance.

- **Will Hetherington,** Editor, Gundog Journal

I have known Jo for a number of years through the LWDG (Ladies Working Dog Group) and love our chats about all things life and dog training. When Jo asked me to read her book, I was super excited to get stuck in and it certainly didn't disappoint! Training your working dog can be a really lonely place and it's easy to get caught up in our own thoughts and feelings. In this book, Jo breaks everything down and helps you navigate the tests and trials of training your working dog and focus on a healthy mindset to achieve the best results for you and your dog. Why has no one written this book before? Having the right mindset is the first step to becoming a successful dog handler. If you have ever trained a working dog or are taking the first steps into training one, then this book should definitely be on your bookshelf. Congratulations on the book Jo and helping yet more people on their training journey

- **Jemma Martin,** Professional Dog Trainer & LWDG Group Expert, Whistle and Wag Dog Training

---

We all have a story to tell, and I fell in love with this one the minute I began reading it. Working with dogs is not a linear process, it's more like a messy ball of wool that we often sit on the ground with and feel overwhelmed by, and wonder if we will ever untangle it? Jo's honest and relatable tales will have you laughing and crying. It's interwoven with the knowledge, skills and experiences she has amassed through her own passions. This book is a reminder to us all that 'we can and we will' find our own happy place with our dogs; it's a compelling and inspired read.

– **Louise Ktoris,** Gundog Influencer, Hawkersbeau Gundogs

It was an honour to be asked to read this book before its publication. I have known Jo for many years now and she is an inspiration to so many ladies and to myself. The Ladies Working Dog Group has brought so many like-minded people together, it is a wonderful community. I know this book will encourage so many owners to keep going, even when things don't always go to plan as expected. This book is easy to read and will give hope to anyone who has ever doubted themselves as a dog handler. I love the real-life examples and the positivity of this book. A must-read!

– **Claire Denyer,** Author of *'The Life Of Rose'*, Professional Dog Trainer & LWDG Group Expert, Family Dog Services

When you're feeling overwhelmed, can't see the wood for the trees or simply don't know where to start, this book is for you. It's the supportive voice that you need when you think you aren't good enough to train your working dog, the encouragement that you need when you feel like you're taking one step forward and two steps back. It's like having a good friend at your side whenever you need it. You'll laugh, you might cry, and you'll most definitely have some light bulb moments - I know I did. I hope that in reading this book you'll realise that you're not alone. Training a working dog isn't always an easy journey but it can be such a rewarding one. Jo gives you the tools to embark and continue on that journey, to keep going when it seems like you're not making progress and to enjoy the ride. Expertly written, Jo's knowledge and personality ensure that The Thoughtful Dog Trainer is a pleasure to read and will be a source of support and guidance for the reader to revisit for years to come.

- **Sue Lister,** Owner of Field and Fireside Ltd.

THE THOUGHTFUL DOG TRAINER

YOUR MINDSET JOURNEY AS A WORKING DOG OWNER

JOANNE PERROTT

authors
AND CO.

First published in Great Britain in 2023
by Authors & Co.
www.authorsandco.pub

ISBN 978-1-915771-40-7 (paperback)

CONTENTS

FOREWORD

I have to say I was flattered when I was asked to write this foreword for Jo, and then daunted and then excited. The reason behind this is that I get to talk to you all directly as to what Jo has brought into my life, and the lives of the tribe I am proud to call myself part of - the Ladies Working Dog Group.

I met Jo when I looked to join the LWDG. I had recently got my first puppy, Scout, that I was looking to train up as a gundog and was daunted and excited about the new journey I had ahead of me. I was immediately bowled over by the openness, honesty and authenticity from the first moment I had contact with Jo. Since then, our relationship has grown and as a senior accredited psychotherapist, I have had the wonderful opportunity to work alongside Jo and the LWDG ladies to bring the human side of psychology into dog training.

Jo is one of the kindest, most tenacious and understanding women I have had the pleasure of coming across in my career and in my life. Her honesty around her health struggles and losing her father never fails to astound me as to how she can turn life's setbacks into personal strength, and I can think of no one better to give a real and human account of the importance of mindset when dog training.

She won't thank me for saying this, but I think it is important it is said - Jo is likely to often brush her skills, her ability, her sheer determination, personal vulnerability and courage under the carpet and for me this book shines her light out and is something she should be very proud of. Over the past few years, Jo and I have laughed together, cried together, ranted together, commiserated, and planned exciting new chapters in our lives, something which I am eternally grateful for. I think we all need a little bit of Jo in our lives and this book is a wonderful way of getting this.

This book isn't all about complex psychological theory, daunting and hard to read. Jo breaks it down into much more accessible and understandable terms. It is as if you are sitting down with a cup of tea and a biscuit in Jo's company and hearing her vast knowledge, experience, strength and encouragement. This is a book for everyone who has ever questioned themselves as a dog handler or needs a bit of a pick-me-up and reframe after a training session that hasn't gone to plan. Allow her words to wash over you. Take what you need and get up and get out again with your dog; the LWDG and Jo are just behind you.

So, I will end by saying, Jo, you lovely lady, I couldn't be prouder of what you have accomplished in this. Love you.

To whoever has picked up this book, if you're passionate about having a great relationship with your working dog and find your self-confidence wavering at times this book is for you.

So, what are you waiting for, put the kettle on, pull up that chair and let Jo do her work.

- **Emma Liddell,** MSc Psych, MBACP (Snr. Accred.), EMDR (accred.) BACP Senior Accredited Psychotherapist, EMDR-accredited trauma therapist, LWDG Mindset Coach.

INTRODUCTION

If you're a working dog owner, you know how challenging it can be to train and find a purpose for your dog. Whether you're training for hunting, competition or simply looking to develop a strong relationship with your pet, the process can be both incredibly rewarding and, at times, massively frustrating.

A working dog in a pet home is a unique blend of companion and athlete. While they still offer the affection and friendship any pet would, they have an intrinsic desire to work and serve. For the owner, this means channelling that energy into productive activities, whether it's basic obedience training, agility courses, cross-country running, scent work or simply long, active walks. The bond between an owner and their working dog is deepened by this shared purpose and activity, making their relationship even more special.

As a gundog owner who has struggled with huge trials and a lack of confidence in my own abilities for a long time, I know first-hand how overwhelming it can be to take charge of your dog's training. That's why I wrote this book, to offer a solution for owners who want to improve their success in training their working dogs.

My aim is to help you gain confidence and develop the attributes needed to train your working dog effectively. Throughout this book, you will find the guidance and the tools needed to build your skills to the stage where your overwhelm can be replaced with confidence. By focusing on your personal growth and development, the result will encourage you to become a positive, successful and knowledgeable dog owner who knows what to do to move forward.

Right now, you might struggle with self-doubt and self-belief when it comes to training your dog. You might feel like you don't know what you're doing or worry that you're not good enough. This leads to frustration and then a lack of progress in training. It can also cause feelings of inadequacy and anxiety, leaving you feeling isolated and unsure of where to turn for help.

But it doesn't have to be this way.

With the right tools and mindset, you can regain control and find success in your training. Your dog is incredibly sensitive to your emotions and body language. If you're feeling uncertain or insecure, your dog is likely to pick up on your feelings and react. By staying calm and confident, you provide a stable environment for your dog to learn in, which helps your dog feel secure and more likely to trust and follow your lead.

When I was a child, my dad used to take me horse riding. He would always say as we rode along, "Jo, there are two minds trying to work as one here, and the one sitting on top is normally the idiot." At the time I didn't think a lot of it, I would just laugh. But as I grew older, I realised that there was a deeper message behind it.

Looking back, I can see my dad was trying to teach me about the importance of working together with our animals, and how it requires a partnership based on trust, communication and respect.

He was reminding me that the owner needs to believe in their capability, no matter what animal they choose to train.

The end of his saying, "the one sitting on top is normally the idiot," is a reminder that as humans, we are all imperfect, and that we need to be humble and self-aware when working with animals. We can't just assume we know what's best, but we need to have strength in our capabilities.

Dad's words have led me to what I do daily in my organisation, helping thousands of female owners to stop feeling overwhelmed and to start building incredibly strong and successful partnerships with their dogs. I've made it my mission to help thousands of women and men just like you to regain control of their lives and their working dogs.

Every dog owner inherently steps into the role of a trainer. Even if not professional, every interaction, command and routine established by an owner shapes their dog's behaviour and understanding of the world. By virtue of daily life together, you teach manners, establish boundaries, and impart social cues, making you an integral trainer in your dogs' life. Throughout this book as the owner, you are also the trainer of which I speak.

Since 2015, when I created the Ladies Working Dog Group, I have helped countless trainers overcome the very same dilemmas you're facing. My qualifications in teaching, as a coach and as a mentor, coupled with years of experience training in the corporate world, have given me unique insights and tools to help you develop the skills needed to become a competent trainer. What we tend to struggle with in our careers and our lives, without doubt, transfers into our dog training.

I'm so excited to help you change your life and training with your dog. I have witnessed the incredible transformations that Ladies Working Dog Group (LWDG) members have undergone by applying the advice and guidance that is available in our community. Through consistent support, many have reported feeling more self-assured and determined, with an increased ability to communicate effectively with their canine companions. They have strengthened their bonds with their dogs and have frequently spoken about a newfound sense of fulfilment and joy in their personal lives. I feel privileged to be a part of their journeys and I'm happy to offer you the same opportunity to discover your true potential as a working dog owner.

I'm thrilled to share my knowledge and experience with you, and to continue to create a community of like-minded owners who are all striving to be the best they can be. By reading this book, you'll not only be helping yourself but also joining me in my mission to empower owners in the working dog world.

Embarking on a new pathway towards personal growth can be incredibly challenging at times - Lord knows how many times I've thought "I'm not good enough for this dog" - and I'm sure you feel like that at times too, but I am here to support you every step of the way. This book is not a quick fix, but rather a guide to refer to, over and over, to help you build the resilience, self-assurance and confidence needed. I understand that the training ahead may be difficult and that's why I am committed to ensuring that we navigate it together in a safe and supportive space.

Too many people are taken out of our amazing sport not through their capability, but through their lack of confidence. Let's take this trip together and come out stronger and more confident on the other side. If you are ready to take the first step towards personal growth and building your confidence, then I invite you to keep reading. Collectively, we can create a happier, healthier and more fulfilling life for you and your dog.

Let's begin...

CHAPTER 1
WHAT AM I EVEN THINKING?

"What the fk am I thinking of, even trying to train these dogs?"**

It's a question I ask myself regularly when I am out with my two English Springer Spaniels. They are both liver and white, with the same size, the same drive and the same determination. But that's where the similarities end.

I bred my girl Ella when Dad was still alive. She was meant to be the dog he taught me to trial, something he loved to do. Ella was the dog that we would take to the top. I owned her mum, Jess. She was a cracking dog and I adored her, just as I love her daughter. Whilst Jess would do anything for me, Ella prefers to make me work hard for it. Every day, she's a reminder of how far I must go to reach that dream Dad and I had of seeing a dog we bred win a trial.

I'm also fortunate to be the proud owner of Rex, a dog of my Uncle Philip's breeding and training expertise. Both my father and his brother, Philip, possess an almost magical kinship with their animals - they just 'get' each other. This ability also echoes in my brother, Ray. I could therefore reason that it is in my genetics, and this surely means I should be the same? Yet I often find myself struggling with my own inhibitions, and spending time, it seems, getting in my own way.

Rex never puts a foot wrong. He's from similar breeding lines to Ella and he's an absolute dream to train. Rex keeps me believing a well-behaved spaniel is an absolute possibility. Rex inspires me to not give up on myself, or on Ella. He reminds me that with perseverance, Ella can be just as good as he is. However, there are days when Ella acts like a cow, not a dog, and Rex's perfect behaviour highlights that I'm probably the weakest link. I didn't train him, he's the result of someone else's skill and dedication. Ella is the result of mine. On these days, I wonder whether I should give up and just forget my trialling dream, and I just want to cry. If you have a working dog, you already understand both the high and low feelings I'm writing about, because it's impossible not to.

There are days when training with both is amazing. I feel like I'm walking on air, and I see a glimmer of hope that one day, I will trial a dog that I have bred and trained, just as Dad and I were working and planning for - a dog with his Afonfelin kennel name becoming a Field Trial Champion. It's these days that recharge my internal battery that keeps me going.

THE PARTNERSHIP BETWEEN YOU AND YOUR DOG

Think about the partnership between you and your dog. You both love each other dearly, of that there is no doubt. But your dog has no real understanding of your reason, your 'why', for building this partnership. If Ella could really understand my every word, if we could sit down and I explain why I want to trial with her, she'd probably say, *"Oh, my god, I didn't know this was so important to you. I will do whatever you need me to, I love you,"*. But she doesn't understand my true emotional motivation, and this is where the issue arises: your 'why' doesn't always align with your dog's choices.

Dogs live in the moment. They don't worry about the past or the future like humans often do. When they play, they are fully in that playtime. When they rest, they are truly resting. The dynamic between your dog's present-oriented nature and your future aspirations creates, shall I say, a fascinating chemistry in the partnership.

Your goal might not be a home-bred Field Trial Champion, it might just be a dog that comes back when you call its name. Maybe your goal is a dog you can take out in public without it making you both look like fools. Whilst these may sound like vastly different desires, they are fundamentally the same - **to have a working dog that works with us and that we are proud of.** A partnership where there are far more happy days than there are teary ones.

To reach this goal, we, of course, need to learn all the dog training skills we can, and I watch in awe as experienced trainers handle their dogs with such ease. But we must also make big changes to our own thinking, who we believe we are and what we believe we can achieve.

This experience is not just about training our dogs, but also about discovering our own strengths and weaknesses, learning to be patient and resilient, and finding the courage to overcome our fears and insecurities.

So, what the fk AM I thinking of, even trying to train these dogs?**

I'm thinking that the process is not only about them but also about me. It's about understanding the true essence of partnership and, in the end, it's about becoming the best version of myself, both for my dogs and for me.

As you embark on this roller-coaster of a ride, you need to understand that setbacks are inevitable. There will be days when everything seems to go wrong, when your dogs don't listen and when you question your abilities as a trainer. But these moments are not reasons to give up; rather, they are opportunities for you to search inside yourself for more. They allow you to reflect on your methods, adjust your approach and find new ways of connecting with your canine partner.

To succeed, you must be willing to invest just as much time and energy into yourself as you put into your dogs. You must be patient, persistent and kind – not just to your dogs, but also to yourself. You must truly understand that there is no such thing as an overnight success in dog training and that true progress comes from a commitment to continuous learning and improvement, and this takes years not days.

Throughout your evolution into a great trainer, it will be essential to celebrate your small victories and to appreciate the progress you make, however small it may be. Each step forward, no matter how irrelevant you may feel it is, is testament to your dedication to your dog and its training.

In the forthcoming days, weeks and months, you must remember that the bond you share with your dog goes beyond any titles, accolades or external validation. It is an attachment formed through love, trust and understanding – a connection that goes beyond the fact you are different species and unites you in a unique and powerful alliance.

So, the next time you find yourself asking, "What am I even thinking?" remember that you're thinking about more than just training your dog. You're thinking about growth, transformation and development of your own mindset. You're thinking about the countless moments of joy and laughter that await you and your smiley-faced, crazy canine breed.

And with each passing day, as you work together, learn together and grow together, you'll find that your dream of a harmonious and successful partnership is not only possible – it's well within your reach.

READER EXERCISE

1. Reflecting on your own experiences as a dog owner can be a key step towards improving. Take a moment to think back on your experiences with your dog so far, both positive and negative. Write down your thoughts and feelings.
2. Consider the times when you felt overwhelmed, frustrated or discouraged, as well as the moments when you felt proud, happy and fulfilled, and write it all down as you work through this book.

FINAL THOUGHTS...

As you've journeyed through this chapter, I hope you've taken a moment to truly reflect on your own thoughts and feelings. Understanding ourselves, our insecurities and our strengths, is so essential, not just for us, but for our dogs as well. As you delve deeper into the upcoming chapters, this self-awareness will be a beacon, guiding your understanding of your dog's needs and behaviours. Remember, every chapter, every lesson, is not just about training - it's about connection, understanding and growth. I'm right here with you, cheering you on every step of the way. You've got this, and your dog is lucky to have someone as dedicated and thoughtful as you by their side.

CHAPTER 2
UNDERSTANDING YOUR IMPACT ON YOUR DOG

Have you ever noticed that the way you think, feel and respond to your dog can have a substantial impact on their behaviour and well-being? Imagine you're preparing for a dog training session. You've had a long, stressful day and you're feeling impatient. As you go through the training exercises, your dog picks up on your tension and responds with nervousness, hesitance or even defiance. He may miss retrieves, refuse to stay, or show other signs of anxiety and confusion.

On the other hand, imagine a day when you come to the training session feeling calm and focused. You give clear and confident commands. Your dog reads and responds to you, following your instructions beautifully, your mood towards them establishing a sort of unspoken understanding between you both that all is relaxed.

This illustrates the power of emotional contagion. Emotional contagion, in layman's terms, is like catching someone else's emotions or mood. Think of it as how you might catch a yawn from someone. If you see someone laughing, you might start to feel happy or even laugh yourself, even if you don't know what they're laughing about. On the flip side, if someone around you is very stressed or sad, you might start to feel a bit of that tension or sadness too, even if nothing sad has happened to you directly. It's the way emotions can spread from person to person without words. Or in this case, person to dog.

This phenomenon is backed by scientific research that highlights a dog's remarkable ability to sense and respond to human emotional cues. Studies have shown that dogs can discern subtle changes in facial expressions, vocal tones and body language, allowing them to gauge their owner's emotional state. This sensitivity forms the foundation for emotional contagion, where a dog's actions reflect the emotional atmosphere set by its handler.

In *Think Dog*, canine behaviourist John Fisher highlighted the deep connection between human and dog personalities in the training process. Fisher wisely suggested in his work,

"We should not only examine the type of dog that we are responsible for; we should also examine what type of person we are before we commence our training."

This insight stresses the importance of self-reflection in dog training. By understanding your own tendencies, strengths and limitations as a trainer, you can design a more effective training plan tailored not just to the dog's needs, but also compatible with your own personality and inclinations.

CONNECTING THE DOTS BETWEEN YOU AND YOUR DOG

It's not always easy to understand the complex, sometimes unseen exchanges between your environment, your thoughts and your emotions, but as a dog owner and trainer, you're constantly navigating this minefield. It's a complicated dance, juggling the interactions between your surroundings, your mental state and your emotions, and it's one you're constantly performing.

Whether you're trying to train your dog to perform new cues or commands, change their behaviour, or simply build a stronger connection with them, the way you approach these tasks can influence the outcomes you achieve.

I am continually fascinated by the relationship between our thoughts and beliefs, our environments and our emotions. All have a profound impact on our lives, shaping our reactions, decisions and, ultimately, our destinies. My time studying psychology at university helped me understand these connections, along with the time I spent studying to be a Certified Canfield Success Principles Trainer. In simple terms, the way we think and feel, can change how we react to things, make choices and shape our lives. We have far more control over our outcomes than maybe we think we do.

I'm especially interested in how our thoughts can be used to help us grow, overcome difficulties and succeed. Through my work, I've always aimed to help people use these concepts to make their lives better. I want to show that by changing how we think and feel about ourselves, we can improve our situations and achieve our goals. This fascination is what keeps me dedicated to helping others reach their full potential and find happiness in whatever it is that's important to them.

In his well-known book, *The Success Principles*, Jack Canfield introduces a big idea: **E + R = O**. This means Event + Response = Outcome. It shows that what happens isn't the only important thing – how we react matters too. We can't control events, but we can control our reactions. Choosing a positive response, even when things are tough, can change the result. This changed how I saw things. This concept has been an eye-opener for many people I've shared it with. People have often found it strengthening to know that they have a say in their outcomes by adjusting their responses, whether in work, relationships, personal growth or dog training.

As I delved deeper into my studies, I encountered the **CTFAR Model** by renowned life coach, Brooke Castillo. This model illuminated how experiences could be dissected into five essential components: Circumstances, Thoughts, Feelings, Actions and Results. Through this model, it becomes evident that our thoughts and responses are pivotal players in shaping the outcomes we experience.

These models together show how closely connected our thoughts and actions are. They point out how important your mindset and behaviour are in shaping where your life goes. By linking your thoughts to what you do, these models reveal how your inside world affects what happens outside. They teach that your thoughts impact the decisions you make and the things you do, which ultimately shape the results you see. This understanding gives us a clear path to making positive changes – by having a mindful mindset and taking purposeful actions, you can guide your life towards a better future.

So, what has this got to do with you and your dog?

E-T-E-R-O^2

As a seasoned dog owner and Founder of the Ladies Working Dog Group, I am also intrigued by how an owner's thoughts and behaviours influence their dog's behaviour and training.

Given the obviously linked nature of a trainer's experience and that of their dogs, I've developed the **E-T-e-R-O^2** © framework. It illustrates how your **environment** triggers certain **thoughts**, which in turn evoke specific **emotions**. These emotions then inform your **response**, which eventually produces your **outcome**.

And this all affects your dog's environment, thoughts, feelings and behaviours, and produces their outcomes.

E-T-e-R-O² is an easy-to-follow framework that will guide you and help you see how these different elements affect one another, and how they play a part in the overall training process.

By understanding and applying this framework, you'll gain a deeper insight into how your state of mind and behaviour can impact your dog, helping you to improve your training methods and improve the quality of your interactions.

Let's identify the parts of this framework:

Environment: This encompasses both the physical surroundings and the social context in which you and your dog interact. It includes the training location, the presence of other people or animals and even external conditions like the weather.

Thought: Perception of the environment triggers thoughts. These mental processes can range from positive and negative to neutral. They act as a bridge between what you observe and how you feel. Remember, while you're processing, so is your dog, albeit in their own, canine way.

Emotion: These are visceral reactions to your thoughts. Negative perceptions might lead to feelings like frustration or anxiety. On the other hand, positive perceptions can cultivate joy, satisfaction, or enthusiasm. All emotions play a role in shaping your interaction with your dog.

Response: Rooted in your emotional state, responses are your reactions to everything around you, including your dog. Frustration might manifest as impatience, whereas contentment often results in patience and positivity.

Outcome: The culmination of this process is the outcome. It's the tangible result of the cascade from environment to response. It's a reflection of your interactions, decisions and emotions throughout the process, offering valuable insights into the effectiveness of your approach and highlighting areas of potential refinement. This outcome isn't just a singular event, it's a mirror to the collective dynamics of environment, thought, emotion and response, and an indicator of the path your training is taking.

By understanding and acknowledging each step in this sequence, you can optimize the training environment and, by extension, the outcomes with your canine companion.

The ² in **E-T-e-R-O²** establishes that both your and your dog's outcomes then feed back into our environment, creating a continuous feedback loop.

If you want to improve your training outcomes and the overall quality of your relationships with your dogs, you need to become aware of this and learn how to influence each part positively.

By mastering the **E-T-e-R-O²** framework, you can become far more intentional in your interactions with your dog. This knowledge can be enabling and provide a foundation for ongoing growth and improvement, not just in dog training, but in every aspect of life.

E-T-e-R-O²

E-T-E-R-O^2 FRAMEWORK – A REAL-WORLD SCENARIO

Training 'Sit' in a Busy Park

Environment (E): Emma decides to train her new puppy, Luna, to 'sit' in the local park. The park, while scenic, is alive with activity: children shrieking as they play, dogs barking and the distant hum of traffic. This bustling environment poses its challenges, as Luna is easily distracted by all the sights and sounds.

Thoughts (T): Emma starts to think, "Maybe this was a bad idea. The park is too noisy. Luna will never learn to sit here, and other trainers will judge my approach." These thoughts set a tone of doubt and apprehension as she begins the training session.

Emotions (e): Stemming from her apprehensive thoughts, Emma starts to feel anxious and frustrated. She's concerned about Luna's progress and whether she's making the right choices as a dog owner.

Response (R): Luna, being a lively puppy, gets easily distracted by a passing butterfly and doesn't respond to the 'sit' command. Given her rising anxiety, Emma's voice grows sharper and her commands more urgent, "Luna, sit! Sit now!" This heightened tension makes Luna concerned and less responsive.

Outcome (O^2): The session doesn't go as Emma hoped. Luna struggles to sit consistently, and Emma feels disheartened. Both leave the park feeling stressed. However, it wasn't just the environment that influenced the outcome; it was the cascade effect of Emma's thoughts, emotions, and reactions in that environment.

Whether you're a new dog owner or a seasoned trainer, understanding the impact of your environment, thoughts, emotions and responses on your dog's behaviour is crucial. These all affect the Outcome **(O).** And you are not the only one being affected by all this, your dog is too, hence the **O^2.**

Fisher, J. (2012). *Think dog.* Cassell Illustrated.

CHAPTER 3
UNPACKING E-T-E-R-O^2

This chapter looks at the E-T-e-R-O^2 framework for dog training in more depth. I'll start with the 'Environment' part.

ENVIRONMENT (E)

The environment is the first stage of the E-T-e-R-O^2. It refers to the external factors and circumstances that we are exposed to, such as our physical surroundings, the people we interact with and the events and situations we encounter. The environment can have a significant impact on our activities.

In dog training, it's important to choose the right environment for your training sessions. This means at the beginning of training, selecting a location that is correct for your dog's capability. Emma, in the previous chapter, would have done better had she chosen somewhere less entertaining. You may need your environment to be free from distractions, such as other dogs or people, which may interfere with your training efforts. A quiet, calm environment can help you and your dog focus on the task at hand and can also promote the positive learning experience that you both need.

However, it's not always possible to control the environment in which you train your dog and sometimes, distractions might be the next sensible step in your dog's progression. As you both grow in your abilities, you may need to change the environment. For example, if you're attending a group training class, you may not have control over the noise level or the behaviours of other dogs in the class. In these situations, it's important to stay focused on your training goals and use the environment as an opportunity.

When choosing a location for dog training, several environmental elements play an important role in determining the session's success. The terrain, whether it's soft grass, hard pavement or sandy surfaces, can significantly influence a dog's comfort and behaviour. Additionally, the acoustics, like distant traffic hums or echoes in confined spaces, can pose distractions, as can strong odours, given a dog's keen sense of smell. The lighting conditions, depending on the time of day and type of illumination, can affect both trainer and canine visibility.

Moreover, unpredictable factors such as wildlife, nearby human activities and even past experiences at a particular location can greatly sway a dog's focus. It's also essential to consider the tools used during training as they become part of the environment.

Weather is another critical component of the environment that can significantly impact your dog training sessions. Whether it's rain, sunshine, wind, or snow, each type of weather condition presents unique issues and also opportunities.

For instance, training on a rainy day may introduce distractions such as mud, puddles and the sensation of raindrops on your dog's fur. While it might be tempting to skip a session due to poor weather, using such conditions can be an opportunity to teach your dog focus and discipline among the distractions.

Conversely, training in excessive heat can be tough on both you and your gundog. It's essential to make sure you both stay hydrated and take regular breaks to avoid getting too hot. You might even want to think about having shorter sessions, either early in the morning or late in the day when it's coolest, to keep everyone safe. If it's really warm out, it's best to skip the training session altogether. Your gundog will thank you.

Similarly, windy days can interfere with your dog's auditory cues, while snowy conditions can introduce a whole new sensory experience for your dog. Each weather condition, while challenging, is an opportunity for you and your dog to learn adaptability and for you to understand and cater to their unique needs in varied environments.

Ultimately, understanding and respecting the weather's influence on the training environment will not only help ensure safety but it also makes the training time better for both you and your gundog. As with all environmental factors, the key is adaptability. The overall temperature and humidity, not just the visible weather conditions, also play a pivotal role in a dog's performance and well-being during training.

In addition to the physical environment, the social environment can also impact your dog's behaviours and training outcomes. This includes interactions with other dogs, as well as meeting up with other people. Dogs are curious, mostly friendly animals, and socialisation is a critical aspect of their training and development. By exposing your dog to different situations in a sensible way, you can help them learn to interact appropriately with other dogs and people and build their confidence. This doesn't mean a free-for-all, chaotic runabout in the park. Your working dog needs you to teach them that the environment they are in shouldn't affect their relationship with you.

A CULTURAL CONVERSATION

In addition to the physical and social environment, the cultural environment can also have a significant impact on a dog's training outcome. This includes people's attitudes towards dogs, dog training methods and the role of dogs in society.

As the Founder of the LWDG, I have the rare opportunity to gain insights into diverse attitudes toward working dogs across various countries, cultures and regions. An area that I've noticed is getting a substantial amount of discussion is the role of gundogs in today's society, particularly in places where hunting is viewed through a controversial lens.

Gundogs, or any dog trained to assist hunters, have an extensive and fascinating history with roots that stretch back to the earliest days of human-canine companionship. Their roles have evolved over centuries, shaping them into incredibly skilled and disciplined animals. These dogs exhibit a remarkable connection with their human partners, a testament to their decades of intense training and instinct.

Gundogs aren't the only dogs that are close to us; other working dogs like sheepdogs are perceived the same way. But there's a difference. Some see gundogs and hunting dogs as tools used for hurting animals, which can cause some arguments. On the other hand, most people see sheepdogs as helpers. It's interesting how we think differently about dogs that are pretty similar at heart.

In some areas, the use of gundogs has become a topic of controversy due to differing opinions about hunting. In regions where hunting with dogs is not considered a necessity, the role of gundogs can be misunderstood or criticised. These dogs can often be subject to misunderstandings or biases associated with the hunting activities they carry out.

It's clear that many gundogs are still used in hunting, but even if you don't plan to use your dog for this purpose, it's important to recognise the complex roles they've had throughout history. Understanding this can deepen your appreciation for your gundog and help you better cater to their unique training needs. Whether you're on a hunting path or not, the rich history and roles of gundogs can make your training journey more meaningful.

Like all dogs bred for specific tasks, gundogs should receive training that nurtures their inherent talents. However, how they are trained varies depending on the owner. They are skilled in various tasks like tracking, flushing out wild game, and retrieving. Some owners choose to use training aids exclusively, while others advance to actual game. Yet, it's important to note that their natural tendencies are what underlie their training. This method enables these working breeds not only to fulfil their roles but also to lead lives that align with their instincts and abilities.

Dogs that go out hunting are far more than mere instruments; they are respected partners, steadily ensuring that hunting is conducted in the most ethical and humane way possible. They thrive on their work, exhibiting pure joy in their tasks. Their well-being is of utmost importance to their trainers and handlers, who invest considerable time and effort into ensuring they are happy and healthy. However, all this history, training and responsibility is lost on those who do not believe that hunting is okay.

For these reasons, it's essential to foster a more informed understanding of gundogs' roles. As with any contentious issue, open dialogue, education and understanding can help shift perspectives and create a more balanced viewpoint on the work these dogs do.

For example, in the United States, hunting dogs are commonly used to source food by families, especially those living in rural areas or regions rich in wildlife. A popular example is in the Midwest, where dogs such as the Coonhound are used for hunting raccoons, a practice that goes back generations.

Raccoons are abundant in the Midwest and provide a source of meat and fur for families. The dogs are specifically trained to track the scent of the raccoons and to tree them, meaning they chase them up a tree where they are easier to hunt.

This partnership between dogs and humans benefits both parties. The dogs are given a job that suits their natural instincts, and their human families gain a reliable method for obtaining food. This age-old practice remains a part of the culture in many rural communities, where sourcing food locally is a way of life and carries a sense of pride and tradition.

This cooperation between humans and dogs is a deep mutual relationship we have developed with dogs over thousands of years. It's a beautiful example of how we've shaped each other's evolution and continue to rely on each other in complex ways.

One of the missions of the Ladies Working Dog Group is to contribute to this conversation, promoting the welfare and understanding of all working dogs, hunting dogs included, amidst varied opinions.

Sometimes you'll meet owners who sadly do see their gundogs only as a hunting tool. They don't care that these dogs have feelings and needs just like any other living being. They miss the whole point of what makes these breeds so special. This lack of understanding can result in them using less effective training methods or applying unnecessary harsh handling, neglect, or even mistreatment.

Dogs form strong bonds with you, and they want to do well, however, employing harsh or abusive training methods can instil fear and confusion in them. Such negative emotions can hold back their learning and compromise the effectiveness of their training.

When we employ a compassionate training approach, it can not only improve a dog's performance but also boost their happiness and health. Training should be founded on respect, free from fear or force. Tailoring our training methods to each dog's specific needs and personality, and providing considerate, non-abusive corrections, assists in the training of the dog while nurturing a relationship of trust. It is essential to remember that there is no "one size fits all" method or approach in dog training.

It is so important to take care of your dogs, even when they're not working anymore. Making sure they have a good life after they retire, keeping them healthy and giving them things to do is just as important as taking care of them when they're working.

As an owner or trainer of gundogs, it's necessary to recognise and address any cultural biases or preconceived notions that could influence your training methods. It's important to educate both yourself and those around you about the distinct attributes and potential of gundogs while fostering a positive opinion of these breeds. By actively addressing and dismantling these cultural barriers, you pave the way for a more inclusive and encouraging community where gundogs can flourish.

HOW THIS ALL TIES TOGETHER

The environment you live in, along with your perceptions of social and cultural norms like those you have thought about whilst reading this, can impact how you train your dog.

Here's how:

1. Contextual Understanding: The environment in which you live provides the setting for your dog's training. It's crucial to understand how to best utilise your surroundings, whether they be urban or rural, to create a conducive learning environment for your dog.
2. Navigating Social Norms: Society and culture play a large role in shaping your attitudes and behaviours. In the context of dog training, societal norms and attitudes can

influence your training and expectations. Being aware of these influences can help you steer them effectively, ensuring a balanced and fair approach to training.

3. Accepting Cultural Perspectives: As a dog owner or trainer, it's crucial to be aware of the cultural assumptions or biases that might impact your approach to training. By acknowledging these influences, you can work to counteract them, leading to a more inclusive and effective training practice.
4. Adapting Your Training Approach: The way you interpret and react to your surroundings, societal norms and cultural attitudes, plays a significant role in shaping your dog training methods. By accepting these factors and how they can influence your approach, you can adapt your training to fit both your and your dog's requirements, leading to more effective and meaningful training outcomes.

ADAPTING TO YOUR SURROUNDINGS

You already adapt your behaviours based on the physical environment around you. Being aware of these differences and how they affect your training approach is essential. Your perceptions can affect your ability to identify and address the situation. Moreover, this adaptability isn't just a reaction but a proactive approach to ensuring your dog's safety and well-being. Different environments come with varied challenges and opportunities, each teaching you and your dog something new. Whether it's mastering the art of patience in a bustling cityscape or enjoying the freedom in the countryside, every setting contributes to your dog's learning experience. As your dog's trainer, your role is to identify these opportunities, harness the positive aspects of each environment, and mitigate potential risks. By doing so, you ensure that your training is not just effective but also tailored to the unique circumstances surrounding you and your dog.

Navigating the Social Environment

What others think can change how you train your dog. You might get nervous if people watch, worried they'll judge if your dog makes a mistake. This worry can make training harder. As an illustration, say, you're teaching your dog to sit in a park and someone comments about how long it's taking, you might feel rushed, but remember, training is a step-by-step journey. It's okay if your dog doesn't get it right immediately. What really matters is moving at a pace that works for your dog, not making other people happy.

One of our LWDG members recently shared a story that many of us can empathise with. She was in the middle of a training session with her gundog at the local park, whistle in hand. Just as she was training, a passerby confronted her, claiming that her use of the whistle was scaring their dog who has a fear of whistles.

Our member was taken aback but remained composed. She explained that she was using the whistle as part of her dog's training and that her primary concern was her own dog's well-being. And her answer was right. Facing public criticism isn't easy. But it's essential to remember—your training choices are yours for a reason. They're designed for your dog's unique needs and to help you achieve your training goals. We train the dog in front of us.

Influences of Cultural and Personal Beliefs

Where you come from can greatly influence how you see and approach dog training. For instance, in some cultures, there's a belief that a strict and disciplined method yields obedient dogs. Imagine a scenario where a dog trainer from such a background uses a whistle and harsh corrections every time the dog misbehaves. On the other hand, other cultures might lean towards gentler, reward-based techniques, where the dog gets a treat for following a command correctly.

Grasping these differences and understanding that there's no single perfect method is crucial. Mixing different techniques, customised to your dog's individual personality, often brings the best outcomes and sets you up as a flexible trainer.

Personal biases and beliefs shaped by your individual experiences affect you, for example, if you've been told that dogs are naturally stubborn, you might approach training with a defeatist attitude. To counter this, you need to recognise your biases and make sure they don't hinder your training.

Understanding all these elements of your environment can help you to become a more effective trainer by altering your next step, which is your thoughts. You can navigate these aspects, balancing caution and freedom, handling social pressure, respecting cultural practices and accepting and addressing your personal prejudices. By doing so, you can provide a well-rounded training environment both internally and externally for your dog, one that respects their unique needs and abilities.

THOUGHTS (T)

In the E-T-e-R-O² framework, the "Thought" part is about how you see and understand the world around you. It's like when you look at something and have a feeling or idea about it. These feelings can be good, bad or just okay. They come from what you believe, what's important to you and things that have happened to you before. To illustrate, if you've always been praised for doing something right, you might feel good when you do it again, but if someone once told you a certain dog breed was tough to train, you might feel unsure when you see that type of dog. These feelings and ideas shape how you react to different situations.

As a dog owner and trainer, it's incredibly important to recognise how your thoughts can impact your interactions with your dog. One example is, if you have negative thoughts about your dog's behaviours, such as "He's stubborn" or "She's untrainable," this can immediately lead to feelings of frustration and disappointment, which in turn can affect your emotions and responses to your dog.

Imagine you once had a dog that loved playing fetch. Now, every time you see a tennis ball, it might make you smile or remember those happy times. On the other hand, if a dog once scared you, you might feel nervous around them, even if they're friendly. This step reminds us that our past can shape the way we think and feel about things today.

It's crucial to challenge negative thoughts and reframe them in a more positive light. For example, instead of thinking "He's stubborn", you can think "He's independent and needs more motivation to follow my commands". Instead of thinking "She's untrainable", you can think "She's a unique individual with her own personality and learning style, and I need to find the right training approach for her".

It's also important to consider how your dog's thoughts and emotions may impact their own behaviours. Your dog is a highly intelligent creature with their own thoughts, feelings and motivations. They too may have negative thoughts and emotions about certain situations or people, which can lead to undesirable actions.

Take, for instance, if your dog has a negative association with a place or noise. They may become anxious or aggressive when exposed to them. Your job here is to think about your own thoughts, which you can control, but also the thoughts of your dog, which you cannot. You can, without doubt, help a dog over time, with training, to alter their thoughts attached to the place or noise, but you cannot change them instantly.

WHEN OUR THOUGHTS DON'T REFLECT REALITY

Our minds are powerful tools that help us find our way in the world, but sometimes, they can play tricks on us. Just like how a small toy can cast a large and menacing shadow on the wall, our thoughts can sometimes magnify or distort what's really happening.

Picture this: you're enjoying a peaceful stroll in the park and unexpectedly stumble over a rock. It's not uncommon for the mind to spiral into self-criticism, thinking, "Why am I always so clumsy?" or "I can't do anything right!" but in reality, it was just a solitary rock on your path. Everyone has these minor missteps; it doesn't mean you're forever bound to trip or that you're always at fault.

Or consider a time when you forgot to do one of your tasks at home. Instead of accepting it as a simple oversight, you might start thinking, "I'm so forgetful, I can't do anything right." This is like seeing one broken window in a house and thinking the entire house is falling apart. But is that one mistake really a sign of your overall capability? Probably not.

These exaggerated thoughts are common and happen to all of us. They can be influenced by past experiences, our upbringing or even just a bad day. However, it's important to remind ourselves that a single event doesn't define the whole story.

Automatic Negative Thoughts (ANTs) are those sneaky and intrusive thoughts that can creep into our minds without conscious effort. These thoughts tend to be negative, self-critical and often irrational, influencing our perceptions and emotions. They are like mental shortcuts that our brains take based on past experiences, fears and insecurities. ANTs can arise from various triggers, such as stressful situations, comparisons or even minor setbacks. For instance, thinking "I'll never be able to do this," or "Everyone probably thinks I'm foolish," are common examples of ANTs. Separating and questioning these automatic negative thoughts is essential for maintaining a healthy mindset and preventing them from dictating our emotions and responses.

When our thoughts seem overwhelming or confusing, it's essential to take a deep breath and give ourselves a moment. Rather than jumping to conclusions about a situation, it's helpful to consider whether what we're thinking is a recurring pattern or just a passing feeling. Sharing our concerns and feelings with a trusted friend can offer clarity. They might provide a fresh perspective we hadn't seen before. Moreover, it's important to take a closer look at our thoughts and consider whether they match up with what's actually happening, the facts of the situation, or if they're more influenced by our thoughts and feelings. It's natural for our internal perceptions to cloud our judgment sometimes, but by taking these supportive steps, we can navigate our thoughts more effectively and align them with reality. Always remember, to better understand yourself is a constant evolution, and every step towards self-awareness is a step in the right direction.

IT'S NOT PERSONAL

We often view the world from our uniquely human perspective, attributing human motivations and emotions to the actions of those around us. This tendency, called anthropomorphism, can lead to misunderstandings, especially when it comes to our pets. Anthropomorphism is when we give human traits or emotions to animals, objects, or even nature. It's like thinking a dog is smiling because it's happy, in the same way humans do, or believing that the clouds are crying when it rains.

Dogs, as with many animals, primarily act based on instinct, learned behaviours and their immediate needs or desires. If your dog digs up your garden or chews on your favourite shoe, it's not an act of rebellion or a personal vendetta against you. Instead, these actions might be driven by a variety of factors such as boredom, anxiety or a simple curiosity.

When you interpret your dog's behaviour as them "being against you" or "doing things on purpose to annoy you", it can damage the bond you share. Not only does this thinking add unnecessary stress and frustration to our lives, but it also hinders effective training and problem-solving. Misunderstanding the root causes of a dog's behaviour may lead to inappropriate or ineffective responses from you.

It's essential to approach your dog's behaviour with empathy and a desire to understand. This doesn't mean excusing negative behaviour but, instead, seeking to comprehend its root cause. If a dog acts in a way that collides with our interests or disrupts our lives, it's rarely, if ever, "on purpose" in the way you might define intent among humans. Their actions are about serving their needs, not opposing ours.

By seeing things from your dog's perspective instead of just a human viewpoint, you build a stronger bond with them. Remember, your dog isn't trying to oppose you; they're simply trying to navigate the world in the best way they know how. By admitting the reality and questioning these kinds of thoughts, you can avoid misunderstandings and be more successful in your training approach.

To be an effective trainer, you must consider both your own thoughts and your dog's thoughts and emotions. You must work to create positive and supportive training conditions that address both your needs and your dog's needs.

EMOTION (E)

As a dog owner and trainer, you probably already understand how emotions can influence your interactions with your dog. Strong emotions such as fear, anger or frustration can make it difficult to train your dog effectively and can even damage your relationship with them. If you become impatient or react out of anger, not only will your training session likely be less constructive, but it can also strain the relationship between you and your dog. On the flip side, positive emotions such as joy, patience and excitement can significantly enhance the training experience. When you approach training with enthusiasm and positivity, your dog can pick up on those vibes. A happy demeanour can make your dog more eager to learn, creating a mutual feeling of accomplishment and connection.

However, it's essential to remember that while our emotions do influence training, they should not dictate it. Balance is key. Overly enthusiastic praise might make a dog overly dependent on constant validation, while excessive negativity can lead to fear and hesitation. Your aim should be to appropriately use your emotions — both positive and negative — in a manner that promotes understanding.

Dogs are highly attuned to your emotional state, so it's important to manage your emotions and consider your dog's emotions during training too. When you experience strong emotions during training, your body responds with physical sensations and behaviours that can affect your dog's behaviour. For instance, if you're feeling frustrated or angry, you might unconsciously tighten your grip on the lead or raise your voice, signalling tension to your dog. Your dog can pick up on these cues.

Creating a positive (but not overly positive) emotional environment during training is essential for achieving success. When a dog feels safe, secure and confident, they're more likely to learn and exhibit the desirable behaviours you want, creating a positive cycle where the dog's good behaviour is rewarded, which reinforces their positive emotional state and encourages more good behaviour.

Dogs' emotions drastically impact their ability to learn and retain training. This is because they can influence a dog's level of focus, receptivity and general behaviour.

Fear or Anxiety: If a dog is fearful or anxious, they're likely to be hyper-alert to potential threats in their environment and less focused on training. An anxious dog might also be hesitant to try new things due to fear of negative consequences, which can make training more difficult. Additionally, fear and anxiety can lead to reactive or aggressive behaviour, which poses significant training barriers.

Excitement: While it's good for a dog to be eager and engaged during training, excessive excitement can also be an obstacle. An overly excited dog may have trouble focusing, may be easily distracted or may engage in undesirable behaviours like jumping up or barking. It's important to channel this energy productively during training sessions.

Stress: Persistent stress can adversely affect a dog's learning capacity. It can trigger health complications, reduce focus and memory, and lead to behavioural problems. However, it's important to distinguish between chronic distress and Eustress, the latter being a positive form of stress that can be beneficial for growth and development. Eustress can contribute to feelings of fulfilment, excitement and meaning. The term was coined by endocrinologist, Hans Selye, comprising the Greek prefix "eu-" meaning "good", and "stress". It's the kind of stress we experience when we are excited about something, such as starting a new job, moving to a new home or going on a vacation.

Eustress can help improve performance and motivation, stimulate creativity, encourage personal growth, and is generally considered to be beneficial or health-enhancing.

For example, in the context of gundog training, a challenging training exercise that is within the dog's ability to accomplish can cause eustress. The dog is stimulated and engaged but not overwhelmed, promoting learning and development.

If a dog is enduring relentless distress, it's crucial to identify and rectify the underlying cause before proceeding with training. While it's key to manage harmful stress, it's equally important not to entirely avoid stress to build a resilient dog. In the right measure, stress can be a vital component of strength and adaptability in dogs.

Happiness and Comfort: A dog who is generally content, feels safe and is comfortable with their trainer, is more likely to be receptive to training. They'll be more focused, more eager to please and more able to absorb and retain new information.

Emotions in dogs, as in humans, are complex and can greatly impact their learning capacity.

CHANNELLING MARY POPPINS IN DOG TRAINING

The world of cinema offers great insights into managing emotions and a classic example can be found in the character of Mary Poppins. Remember the scene where she magically tidies up the children's room? With a snap of her fingers, toys put themselves away and the room transforms from chaos to order. Her calm and composed demeanour, paired with a touch of magic, turned a typically frustrating task into a delightful experience.

Imagine applying the "Mary Poppins approach" to dog training. Instead of getting upset when your dog doesn't immediately obey a command or behaves in an unexpected manner, keep calm and use positive reinforcement. Much like how Mary uses her magical touch and gentle firmness to guide and correct the children, we too can make our training sessions delightful by channelling Mary Poppins-like positive emotions and patience.

While Mary Poppins brought an air of enchantment to every situation, she was by no means a pushover. The children quickly learned that beneath her cheerful disposition and magical tricks lay a strong, no-nonsense attitude. She was firm in her convictions and stood her ground when needed. She understood the importance of boundaries, and she made sure the children understood them too.

Similarly, effective dog training is not about letting your dog do as they please. It's about setting clear boundaries and being consistent in enforcing them. Like Mary Poppins with the children, you need to be the guiding force in your dog's life, providing structure and stability. This doesn't mean being harsh or punishing, but rather using positive reinforcement to reward desired behaviours and gentle corrections for undesired ones.

The key is balance. Mary Poppins could be strict, but she was also deeply caring and knew when to use her unique brand of magic to lighten the mood. You must find that emotional balance between firmness and kindness. Dogs, much like children, thrive in an environment where they understand the rules and know they are loved. Channelling your inner Mary Poppins means recognising when to be firm and when to be gentle, and always approaching training with a sense of compassion and understanding.

Of course, we can't literally snap our fingers to make our dogs obey, but with the right emotional balance, our training can seem just as miraculous. Taking a page from Mary Poppins' book, we're reminded that with a spoonful of patience and a dash of joy, even demanding tasks can become opportunities for growth.

RESPONSE (R)

When it comes to dog training, your responses to your dog's behaviour can have a significant impact on the outcomes you achieve. The Response (R) stage of the **E-T-e-R-O²** framework refers to the actions you take in response to your thoughts, emotions and environment. By understanding and managing your responses effectively, you can achieve huge steps forward.

Acknowledging your own emotions is a vital aspect of managing the Response (R) stage of the **E-T-e-R-O** ² framework in dog training. By addressing your own feelings in a healthy and positive manner, you can effectively handle your reactions to your dog's behaviours and achieve improved outcomes. When you address your dog's behaviours, it's important to do so in a constructive and positive way. This involves avoiding knee-jerk responses that arise from anger, frustration or impatience, as these can negatively impact the connection you've developed with your dog. Instead, aim to approach each situation with comprehension and patience. For example, if your dog doesn't follow a command, it might not be because of stubbornness or defiance. There could be various reasons, like confusion, distraction or a partial understanding of the instruction.

Another important aspect of the Response stage is consistency. Consistency in your responses helps your dog understand what is expected of them, which leads to better outcomes. Inconsistency can be confusing and frustrating for your dog, which can lead to unwanted behaviours and poor outcomes.

The importance of the timing and appropriateness of your responses cannot be overstated.

A timely response plays a crucial role in creating a clear connection in the dog's mind between its behaviour and your reaction. It's all about the immediacy - if your dog sits on command and you reward it promptly, it will associate sitting with the reward. If you delay the reward, the dog might not understand why it's being rewarded, leading to confusion. This concept is known as "event contiguity", a term used in psychology to describe the close timing of two events that helps establish an association in the mind.

EVENT CONTIGUITY AND REWARDING

Timing is everything in dog training. The concept of event contiguity teaches us how important it is to closely link two events so your dog makes the connection in their mind. It's rooted in the theory of classical conditioning, famously demonstrated by Ivan

Pavlov's experiments. Pavlov's dogs were accidentally conditioned to associate the sound of a bell with mealtime. The study was a study on digestion.

Initially, the dogs would salivate only when they saw or smelled their food. Pavlov began to ring a bell just before presenting the food. Over time, the dogs started to salivate at the sound of the bell alone, anticipating the food that usually followed. This learned response demonstrated that behaviours could be conditioned, or learned, through association.

Pavlov's work with his dogs forms the basis of many training techniques used today. We condition dogs to associate our commands ("sit", "stay", "come") with specific actions. Through consistent reinforcement – praise, treats, or toys when they perform the correct action – they learn to respond to these commands.

This is an application of Pavlov's principles of classical conditioning, showing that his work remains as relevant and useful today in dog training as when it was first conducted.

Applying this to your dog training, if your dog sits on command and is immediately rewarded, it will associate sitting with a positive outcome, be it a treat, praise or playtime. If the reward comes too late, your dog may not connect the behaviour with the reward, leading to confusion and slower learning.

As time passes and you consistently offer timely and appropriate responses, your dog will learn to associate positive behaviours with rewards and less desirable actions with a lack of rewards. This will result in a well-trained dog that understands what is expected and feels secure and confident in its interactions with you.

LWDG Group Expert, Claire Denyer, always emphasises the importance of "paying your dog for a job". She believes that rewards are an integral part of training, like putting "money in the bank". When your dog performs a task correctly or behaves in a desired way, it's essential to reward them promptly. This reinforces the behaviour, making it more likely to occur again. It's an investment in your dog's learning, steadily building a "bank" of positive associations and behaviours. With every reward, you're depositing "money" into this bank and the "interest" is a well-trained, responsive and happy dog.

COMMUNICATION AND RESPONSE

The open line of communication established during the Response (R) stage of the E-T-e-R-O^2 framework is fundamental to its success. This stage plays a crucial role in enabling an understanding between you and your dog, acting as the bridge that links your commands to your dog's comprehension of them. By ensuring your responses are timely, consistent, and appropriate, you are effectively 'speaking' a language that your dog can understand, thereby enhancing the efficiency of the communication.

This heightened level of understanding has the potential to significantly improve the overall effectiveness of the E-T-e-R-O^2 framework. It results in a training experience that is not only more successful but also more positive for both parties involved. Your interactions with your dog become less about command and obedience, and more about shared understanding and cooperation.

The beauty of this approach lies in the fact that it goes beyond training and extends into the very relationship you share with your dog. It instils a sense of confidence in your dog, as they learn to navigate their world.

Moreover, this approach cultivates a state of happiness and contentment in your dog. When your dog knows what is expected and how to meet those expectations, it reduces anxiety and uncertainty, leading to a happier, more relaxed pet. This mutually beneficial understanding and coexistence create a harmonious relationship that is the overall goal of the E-T-e-R-O^2 framework. It transforms the dynamic from one of mere pet and owner to a team that understands, trusts, and respects each other.

OUTCOME (O)

The Outcome (O) stage of the E-T-e-R-O² framework refers to the result of your responses and reactions. The outcome can be positive or negative, depending on the effectiveness of your responses and the external factors at play. When it comes to dog training, the outcome can range from simple tasks like sitting on command to more complex tasks like retrieving games.

Think of training like building a house: each brick matters. Every time you interact with your dog, you're adding another brick. The quality of the materials (your training methods and responses) will dictate the strength of the house (the outcome). It's not just about correcting wrong behaviours but also rewarding the right ones.

Imagine teaching your gundog the "Stop to Flush" technique. This is a training process where you want your dog to immediately stop and remain stationary once it has flushed a bird, rather than giving chase.

Scenario A: In your initial training outings, your gundog excitedly locates and flushes a bird from its hiding spot but can't resist the temptation to chase it. If, in frustration, you shout or become visibly upset when the dog returns, the dog might start linking the act of flushing a bird with a negative outcome. The result? The dog might either become reluctant to engage in flushing at all, or it might do so with visible signs of stress, anticipating the scolding that follows.

Scenario B: Alternatively, during your training, you decide to equip yourself with a whistle and some treats. Each time your dog successfully flushes a bird and then stops on its own or upon your command, you reward the behaviour with a treat or vocal praise. However, if the dog gets carried away and chases after the bird, a sharp whistle becomes your tool to recall and redirect its attention back to you. Gradually, the dog starts associating the act of flushing and then pausing with a positive reward. The outcome? A well-trained gundog that not only excels in the "Stop to Flush" technique but also eagerly looks to you for the next command, knowing that good behaviour leads to positive reinforcement.

Getting good results in training your dog needs the right responses, being consistent and having patience. It's important to set rules and limits and correct your dog in a suitable way. This helps your dog know which behaviours are good and which are bad. Also, having achievable goals and celebrating little wins can keep you and your dog excited and this helps get more good results. These parts of training help it to work better and be more enjoyable.

A NEEDED NOTE ABOUT CORRECTION

I truly believe, as do our group experts, in the importance of gentle but firm correction when training dogs. Sadly, many dogs, especially young male dogs reaching adolescence, end up in rescue centres when this kind of training is missing.

When dogs reach adolescence, they start to test limits and find out who they are, just like people do. Without the right guidance during this time, these dogs can start to act out and become hard to handle. If they don't have clear rules or a strong bond with their owner where they listen to and understand each other, things can get even worse. In the end, the owner might feel they have no choice but to rehome their dog. This is a heartbreaking situation that could have been avoided with the right training and communication from the start.

Constructive correction, as opposed to harsh handling, is an essential part of effective dog training. Constructive correction involves guiding the dog towards the desired behaviour in a gentle yet firm manner. It allows the dog to learn from its mistakes without feeling threatened or scared.

This type of correction nurtures a positive learning environment, building trust and understanding between the dog and the handler. Harsh handling, on the other hand, can lead to fear and confusion, hindering the learning process and your relationship.

With constructive correction, dogs are more likely to comprehend the desired behaviour, feel confident and be motivated to learn, resulting in a successful and well-behaved dog.

While this book aims to assist the owner rather than focusing on dog training, I understand that you may be facing huge problems in your training sessions with your dog right now. If this is the case, I want to tell you that free advice and support is available. You can listen to our free podcast, 'Found It. Fetched It', on most podcast platforms, or explore our free resources on our website.

Additionally, you can join our membership to gain access to the wisdom of our exceptional experts, all of whom are experienced gundog trainers who employ similar methods, including the use of appropriate correction. There is so much valuable training support available that will give you the skills needed to overcome the obstacles that you may be facing.

I also want to clarify that the term "correction" can mean very different things in different parts of the world. In the context of this book and throughout our organisation, when we mention 'correction', we are referring to kind, non-harsh, suitable correction that aids the dog's learning. We do not advocate for harsh handling or punitive measures. Instead, our focus is on fostering a positive learning environment where the dog feels supported and understood, which ultimately leads to a successful training experience.

THE CYCLICAL NATURE OF E-T-E-R-O ^{2}

E-T-e-R-O ^{2} is a cyclical framework that emphasises the dynamic interactions between your environment, thoughts, emotions, responses and outcomes in dog training. It basically goes round and round, the outcome changes the effects of the environment, be it a small physical change or a huge change in your thoughts.

It's important to recognise that this is not linear or one-directional; rather, it's a constant feedback loop that involves both the trainer and the dog at different stages and in different ways.

The squared sign in E-T-E-R-O ^{2} represents the fact that both the trainer and the dog are involved in the process and it's important to take note that may not be at the same stage or level of the cycle. Just as in a dance, each partner has their own steps and rhythm, so too, in training, the trainer and the dog might find themselves at different stages of understanding or execution.

Let's use the example of chasing a rabbit. Whilst the trainer may be experiencing negative emotions such as frustration or impatience, the dog may be feeling happy and self-rewards by chasing a bunny. The trainer might be in the 'Response' stage, thinking they have given a clear command to stop, but the dog might still be in the **Emotion** stage, processing the excitement of a dashing dinner. This cycle is dynamic, and both parties don't always move in tandem. Knowing this helps you become more compassionate, watchful, and adaptable. This way, you both can move forward together through the ups and downs of training.

Understanding the cyclical nature of E-T-e-R-O ^{2} is critical for valuable training. It means recognising **that each stage of the framework both influences and is influenced by the other stages**, and that progress may require revisiting and revising earlier stages. In other words, if a trainer is not achieving the desired outcome in their dog's behaviours, it may be necessary to revisit their thoughts and emotions about the situation and adjust their responses accordingly.

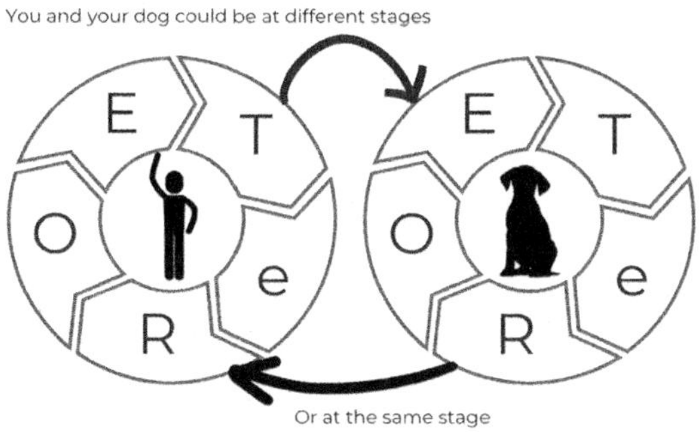

E-T-e-R-O²

Understanding your dog's needs through the E-T-e-R-O ² cycle is like having a two-way conversation without words. This framework reminds us that training is a tango between you and your dog, where both are constantly learning and adjusting. Let's say you're teaching your dog to sit. If they seem distracted or anxious, it might not be stubbornness, but perhaps something in the environment is bothering them. By being aware of their emotional state and adjusting your approach or the surroundings, you can address their needs. This cycle encourages a partnership where both you and your dog work together, adjusting and learning from each other's cues. This ongoing conversation ensures a happier and more effective training and life for both of you.

If Dad read this chapter he'd laugh and say, "There are two minds trying to work as one here," identifying the connection between the stages of the E-T-e-R-O ² Framework. This is a humorous but accurate way to describe the active, always-moving, always-changing relationship between you and your dog. When working with your dog, it's important to remember that both you and your dog are actively participating in training, not just one of you.

CHAPTER SNAPSHOT:

- **ENVIRONMENT:** Be mindful of the environment in which you train your dog and choose a location that is free from distractions and promotes a positive learning experience. Consider how the social and cultural environment may impact your dog's behaviour and training outcomes.
- **THOUGHTS:** Challenge negative thoughts and reframe them in a more positive light. Consider your dog and work to create a positive and supportive training environment that addresses both of your needs.
- **EMOTION:** Manage your own emotions and consider your dog's emotions during training. Create a positive emotional environment that builds trust and a stronger bond between dog and trainer.
- **RESPONSE:** Respond to your own feelings in a healthy and positive way and respond to your dog's behaviours in a constructive and rewarding way. Be consistent in your responses to help your dog understand what is expected of them.
- **OUTCOME:** Set realistic goals and celebrate small successes along the way. Focus on achieving positive outcomes by combining effective responses, consistency and patience.

READER EXERCISE

Keep a diary for the next seven days where you identify where you are and where you think your dog is on the cycle.

Beginning a reflective diary can offer great insights into the dynamics of your relationship with your dog, specifically how your emotions and actions affect each other. Let's delve into a more detailed plan for keeping this diary over the next week.

1. Daily Observations: Each day, set aside some time to reflect on your interactions with your dog. It could be right after a training session or at the end of the day. Write about what happened, what you did and how your dog responded. Make note of any changes in behaviour, mood or attitude from both you and your dog.
2. Evaluate Your Emotions: Identify and record your emotional state at different points throughout the day, especially during interactions with your dog. Were you stressed? Relaxed? Happy? Frustrated? Also, attempt to discern your dog's emotional state based on their behaviour and body language.
3. Impact on Each Other: Reflect on how your emotions and behaviour may have influenced your dog's actions and vice versa. For instance, if you were feeling stressed or distracted, did your dog seem more restless or less responsive to commands?
4. Training Sessions: Pay special attention to your training sessions. How did your emotional state affect your approach to training, your patience level or your reaction to your dog's behaviour? Observe how your dog reacts to your training cues and commands. Are they eager? Indifferent? Anxious?
5. Identifying Patterns: As you record your observations over several days, start to look for patterns or correlations. Do

you notice that your dog is more responsive or well-behaved when you're calm and confident? Conversely, do they seem more anxious or less cooperative when you're stressed or impatient?

6. Actionable Steps: Based on your observations, start to identify ways you can enhance your interactions and training sessions with your dog. Perhaps you need to work on staying calm and patient, even if your dog isn't picking up a new command right away. Or maybe you need to try to ensure your dog feels relaxed and confident before starting a training session.

Remember, the goal of this diary is not to judge or criticise, but to gain a deeper understanding of the mutual influence you and your dog have on each other. The insights you gain from this exercise can help you adapt your training strategies and improve your relationship with your dog.

FINAL THOUGHTS...

I want to share something invaluable with you. The beauty of the E-T-e-R-O² framework is its interconnectedness. Picture it like a dance - when one step falters, you can always adjust another to maintain your rhythm. So, if ever you find yourself caught in the challenge of managing your feelings during training, take a moment. Redirect those thoughts. You'd be surprised how such a shift can change your whole interaction with your beloved pet, leading to outcomes you both cherish.

If the results aren't lining up with what you hoped for, that's okay. It's an opportunity to look at your actions, make tweaks and keep going. Consistency and patience, I promise you, will make all the difference.

The E-T-e-R-O² framework isn't a one-time fix but an evolving guide to effective training. It's natural to hope for immediate results but remember that the best things often take time. What's most important is the joy you find in each training session, the bond you deepen and the journey you share with your dog. Together, with patience and understanding, you're laying down the groundwork for lasting success. And always remember, I'm here cheering you on.

Canfield, J. (2005). *The Success Principles (TM)* - 10th Anniversary Edition: How to Get from Where You Are to Where You Want to Be. HarperCollins Leadership.

Castillo, B. (2008). *Self-Coaching 101*. Futures Unlimited Coaching.

Pavlov, I. P. (1927). Conditioned reflexes: An investigation of the physiological activity of the cerebral cortex. London: Oxford University Press.

CHAPTER 4
LEADING WITH DETERMINED DOGGEDNESS

Owners who are good at training working dogs share two main traits: they manage rewards well and they hang out with their dogs, lots.

Firstly, they use rewards like treats or praise wisely. This helps the dogs learn good behaviour. By giving rewards at the right times, trainers make sure the dogs stay interested and eager to learn.

Secondly, they spend time playing and talking with their dogs. Working dogs need lots of activity and attention. When trainers interact with their dogs through training and communication, they build a strong connection. This connection makes the dogs more likely to listen and follow instructions.

Both of these are going to take you time, the first to develop the skill of rewarding correctly and the second, time on the clock face. Whether it's two minutes in the kitchen training whilst the kettle boils, or two hours in a wood working on hunting patterns, you are going to need to be incredibly invested in getting this right. Anything that takes time also needs you to keep going and never give up. One of the most important attributes you'll need is determined doggedness.

It's no secret that training and working with your dog can swing between being massively rewarding and incredibly frustrating. The ultimate victory for many of you is in building a strong bond of companionship and partnership, where your dog promptly responds to cues. But what happens when the unavoidable hurdles crop up, when doubts begin to murk your vision and frustrations start tethering your progress?

This is where the strength of your spirit really stands out.

Developing resilience is essential for any working dog owner who wants to build a strong, positive relationship with their dog and succeed in their training journey. By building up your mental and emotional strength, you can face any obstacle that comes your way with confidence and determination. **And the challenges will come.** With a puppy, it can seem like an hourly battle. With an adolescent dog, it can seem constant.

And whilst they are causing chaos, you are trying to work out what on earth to do. And that's because, quite honestly, if this is your first or second dog, your dog training skills are probably still in their early stages.

You see, dog training is an art that's often honed over time and through hands-on experience. Much like learning to play a musical instrument or mastering a new language, becoming proficient in dog training doesn't happen overnight. It's a skill set that grows and improves over time with practice, patience and a whole lot of trial and error.

When you're a first-time dog owner, you're just beginning to navigate this complex world. Everything is new, from understanding your dog's unique signals and behaviours to learning how to respond to them in a constructive manner. You're still finding your footing, trying to work out the best training methods and adapting to the highs and lows that come with this role. This uncharted territory can undoubtedly shake your confidence at times, especially when things don't go as planned.

If this is your second, third or even your fourth dog, although you may have some foundational experience, each dog is unique and presents its own set of struggles.

Just like humans, no two dogs are the same. The methods that worked perfectly with your first dog might be less effective with your second. You're learning all over again, in a sense, and this time with a completely different individual. This can test your confidence, causing you to massively second guess your training abilities.

All in all, it's entirely normal to find yourself in at the deep end of your early experiences of dog ownership. It's a relationship that requires time, patience and perseverance, and the learning curve can sometimes be steep. So, when you're dealing with a constant barrage of new difficulties, it's natural to feel overwhelmed and question your capabilities. The key is to remember that like all things, mastery comes with time and experience, and each hurdle is just another stepping stone to becoming a competent dog trainer.

And let's not overlook something crucial—you're already skilled at pushing through when times are tough. So, if you're still getting the hang of training your gundog, don't worry. You're already equipped with the strength and perseverance you'll need to succeed.

HARNESSING YOUR INNER STRENGTH

Resilience is a quality that you've likely developed in various aspects of your life, and it can, without doubt, be applied to your dog training experiences. In many ways, the resilience you've built in other situations, like learning to sit through the fifth night of your child's school play and still smile, can serve as a transferrable skill that will get you through the hardest moments with your dog. Think about it. All through life, you've faced different problems, right?

Consider the times you have overcome personal setbacks, such as losing a job, ending a relationship, or dealing with health issues. Bouncing back from these situations required stamina, and you can channel that same strength and determination into facing setbacks with your dog.

In dog training, you'll be constantly learning new techniques and strategies to help your dog succeed, and the grit you've built from your past problems will help you persevere.

Think for a moment about the friendships with others you have created and kept. Some have taken bucketloads of inner strength. I'm sure you have met all sorts of people, all with their own ways of talking and sometimes, you might have even disagreed with them, but you still like them. The same kind of patience and determination you've used to build these friendships can help you when building a relationship with your dog. Trust, understanding and endless patience are just as important with our four-legged friends as those with two.

By reflecting on these life experiences and the resolve you've developed, you can tap into this strength when you're feeling frustrated or overwhelmed in your dog training journey.

I have seen so many examples of how a handler's determination has helped in their dog training. For instance, I know a fantastic woman who took on two rescue working dogs at the same time, and every time I talk to her, she shows an incredible resilience to the training challenges she has faced, and those still to come. Her once worried face has changed into a proud one. And rightly so, she has done a fantastic job with both dogs. They once were hesitant and unsure but have transformed under her guidance. The training wasn't without its bumps, but her unwavering determination was evident at every turn. Every setback became an opportunity for growth and every small success was celebrated. Her progress is a testament to the power of human perseverance and the deep union that can form when dedication meets love. Her story is a shining example that, with the right mindset and commitment, even the toughest obstacles in dog training can be conquered.

USING RESILIENCE TO OUR ADVANTAGE

Throughout my personal evolution, I've found that my bounce-back ability has been instrumental in overcoming my own insecurities and self-doubt as a dog owner. The nagging feeling of being an imposter, of not being up to the task, has been a frequent companion throughout my progression. Yet, time and again, my ability to quickly recover has acted as my safety net, catching me when I've stumbled and propelling me forward with renewed vigour. Each setback, whether it was a training mishap, a misunderstood cue or a moment of sheer frustration, became less about failure and more about growth. Instead of dwelling on my mistakes, I learned to embrace them as valuable lessons.

When my father passed away, this attitude seemed to be needed at every moment. At the time, my spaniel Ella was just a little over a year old and she was headstrong, with a mind of her own. She didn't listen and honestly, I was at a loss about where to begin. The ever-reliable guiding hand of my father was no longer available.

During the prolonged, harrowing months when we were struggling with my father's illness, the care for all our dogs had been reduced to the bare essentials. Gone were the hours of training and devotion. Ella was fed, given water and taken for walks – but that was it. The joy, the playfulness, the fun that should be an integral part of any dog's life had been largely absent, replaced by the grim reality of our family's ordeal.

Then, with Dad gone, I was faced with the task of training Ella, who had adapted to a lifestyle that seemed perfectly fine without my active participation. The struggle of reintroducing myself into Ella's life, to become more than just the person who provided her basic needs, was daunting. But this was where resilience came into play. I had to draw on my inner strength, lean into the discomfort, and begin forging a deeper, more meaningful bond with Ella.

It would have been very easy to give up right there and in all honesty, the weight of the world made that option very tempting. Left with all of Dad's dogs to rehome, my heart was breaking with every decision I had to make. The quiet promise I had whispered by his bedside, assuring him that I'd always take care of them all haunted my every step. Guilt became a heavy shadow, constantly reminding me that I hadn't kept my word. I felt like a complete failure, especially when thoughts of abandoning my passion for gundogs altogether crossed my mind.

After losing my anchor, the daunting responsibility of what lay ahead, paired with my existing struggles with Ella, felt like too much. The world of gundogs, which once brought so much joy and purpose, was now a painful reminder of the void left behind by my father's absence.

Yet, that's where my bounce-back ability, honed over years of setbacks, became indispensable. Instead of wallowing in the overwhelming sorrow and guilt, I decided to turn these emotions into driving forces. Each dog I managed to rehome was a testament to my commitment to honouring my father's legacy long-term; sure, I couldn't keep them all, but I could keep some and, more importantly, I could keep going.

And with Ella, it wasn't just about training but also healing. We became each other's support. Every session, every walk, every moment of understanding became a silent tribute to him and the love he had for all his dogs.

Though the path was filled with so many heart-breaking memories, it was the resilient spirit he had instilled in me, along with my mum, which guided me through the darkest times, reminding me of the love, passion, and commitment that had always defined my relationship with gundogs.

Steering through the world of dog training, you'll invariably encounter hurdles, be it training hiccups, behavioural quirks or juggling the demands of work and family life alongside your canine commitment. Yet, it's your underlying tenacity that becomes your compass, guiding you to confront these barriers directly. Anchored in that determination, your training will evolve into a steadfast pursuit of cultivating an enduring friendship with your dog.

It's not uncommon for people to feel anxious or uncertain about the 'right' or "best' way to train their dogs, particularly if they've previously had challenging or disappointing experiences, but with your perseverance, you can change this. Training sessions that are going badly can feel so long and challenging, and staying focused and motivated throughout the process can be difficult. Remind yourself that you have overcome setbacks before and can do so again. Adapt your approach, learn from your mistakes and continue moving forward. This unwavering focus, in turn, will help you create a more productive training environment.

So how do you find the courage to keep going?

ENDURING THROUGH DIFFICULT TRAINING PHASES

Training will often hit difficult stages, such as when you are teaching your dog a new command that they're not getting, maybe you're encouraging steadiness or entering new environments to improve your training. It can be incredibly tempting to give up when progress seems slow or non-existent, however, your growing willpower can help you through these problematic phases and see the struggles as opportunities for growth.

Imagine you're trying to teach your dog the "stop" command, but they just don't seem to understand what you want from them. Instead of becoming frustrated or giving up, you could try different approaches to communicate the command more effectively. Perhaps using a different tone of voice, incorporating hand signals, using a different training method or breaking the command down into smaller steps might make it easier for your dog to grasp the concept.

Another example could be when introducing your dog to new environments, such as a busy city centre, where they might feel overwhelmed and anxious. You remain patient and empathetic towards your dog's needs, allowing you to gradually desensitise them to the new surroundings at a pace they're comfortable with.

By staying calm in these moments, you'll promote a deeper understanding of your dog's unique learning style and temperament, assisting you to further tailor your training techniques to best suit their needs.

THE BENEFITS OF NOT GIVING UP

It's not uncommon when training your dog to feel like you're in over your head or that you don't know what you're doing. When you undoubtedly encounter training setbacks, it's totally natural to feel incredibly stressed. However, if you don't learn to cope with these feelings, they can quickly spiral out of control and lead to more serious issues between you and your dog.

Running into problems and obstacles is normal. **These bumps in the road are valuable chances for you to grow stronger.** When you tackle and beat these issues, you're building up your mental and emotional strength. This doesn't just help you handle future problems better, but also reinforces the skills you need for success, teaching you exactly how to deal with stress and adversity healthily and proactively, rather than becoming overwhelmed and spiralling into negative thought patterns about how you are destroying the dog in front of you rather than training it.

With help, you can learn to reframe negative experiences as opportunities for growth and learning rather than becoming overwhelmed by them.

When I first started training my first gundog pup, it was tough. I was learning new skills alongside already dealing with severe anxiety from my health worries, which made the stress even worse. Every day felt like a battle, and I wasn't sure I had what it would take to succeed.

I found it so difficult at the beginning because both the dog and I were learning new skills and behaviours. The dog did not understand what was expected of it and I struggled to communicate what I wanted my dog to do. On reflection, it was an incredibly frustrating experience for both of us.

You know that saying, "the blind leading the blind"? It was so true when it came to us trying to work together. It was a recipe for confusion, mistakes, and frustration. That's why I sought the guidance of experienced and knowledgeable people to help me navigate the way.

The learning curve was incredibly steep, and I made many mistakes along the way. I would get irritated when things didn't go as planned or when my dog wasn't responding the way I wanted it to. There were times when I wanted to give up so badly, but I knew deep down that if I did, I'd lose the fantastic times that could be had with my dad, out on an estate with an obedient dog that I had trained myself.

Over time, I started to develop the doggedness needed to keep going. It didn't happen overnight; it took years of practice and patience to get to where I am today, and I still have so far to go. I have had to learn to push through setback after setback and keep working towards my goals, even when it feels like I'm making no progress.

I've learned that dog training is not a sprint, but a marathon. It wasn't a transformation that occurred in a day or a week, instead, it's taken years of diligent practice, stubborn patience and an untiring commitment to reach the point where I am today. And even with all the strides I've made, I recognise that I still have a significant amount of learning ahead of me. The reality is that just when I think I've found my footing, life can sometimes throw another curveball my way. It can feel like just when I've scaled one hill, another, taller one, is waiting for me.

In August 2022, I was hit with the devastating news that my brain tumour had returned for the third time. This was a major setback, a colossal hurdle that threatened to derail all the progress I had made. I had been told for the previous five years that I was clear of any regrowth, and I'd started to relax that my brain tumour had gone completely, and the nightmare was all over. Then, in a single sentence in a letter from my consultant, I was devastated. There was a tumour on my scan.

Dealing with this meant that my focus and energy were totally diverted from my dog training. I found myself at a standstill, fighting with the uncertainty of my health situation, while also trying to maintain my connection with my dogs. It was a challenging time, to say the least.

Getting back on track following such a significant personal crisis has been no small feat. It's required immense strength and a massive conscious effort to reclaim the progress I had made before my diagnosis.

I've had to relearn certain skills, rebuild my stamina and perhaps most importantly, reignite my confidence. I've had to constantly remind myself of the strength I had developed over the years and trust in my ability to bounce back.

I've also had to adjust my expectations, knowing that there will be days when it seems like I'm making no progress at all. On these days, it's easy to feel stuck in a rut, with my training efforts producing no tangible results. But I've learned to push through these periods of inactivity by just doing the smallest of actions. I remind myself that every step, no matter how small, is a step forward. I understand that setbacks and issues, whilst frustrating, are part of my growth, shaping me into a stronger, more capable version of me.

There are undoubtedly more trials ahead, but I remain committed. With every delay I overcome, I not only become a more skilled dog trainer, but I also reinforce my own inner strength, further preparing me to face whatever life may throw at me next. And there will always be a 'next', for all of us.

There's a powerful adage that was once shared with me, a simple phrase that has since etched itself into the very fabric of my perspective: after every breakdown comes a breakthrough. At first, I thought this was just a way to make people feel better, but over time, I've seen it's true. When things fall apart, we're forced to really look at ourselves, to think about what matters most. This can be a bit of a wake-up call, helping us see things more clearly. And often, it's after these tough times that we find new ways to move forward, stronger and wiser. This idea has given me a lot of hope, especially when things get rough. I've learned to be kind to myself, to take breaks when I need them and to keep pushing forward. While the road ahead may be difficult, the rewards and satisfaction of seeing progress in training make it all worth it in the end.

DEVELOPING HEALTHY COPING STRATEGIES FOR STRESS

Developing healthy coping strategies for stress is crucial in facing the problems of dog ownership. One way that helps you cope with stress is by increasing your self-esteem. As you learn to trust yourself and your abilities to handle difficult situations, you develop a greater sense of self-worth and confidence.

Successfully teaching your dog a new behaviour or skill can fill you with a sense of accomplishment and pride in both you and your dog. This uplifting feeling can help reinforce your belief in your ability to succeed through your hard work and dedication. By focusing on your accomplishments and your growth over time, you can draw on your resilience to build healthy coping strategies for stress.

Looking back on your journey as a dog owner can help you recognise the progress you have made, and the skills and strategies you have developed to overcome the obstacles you face. Drawing on your past success can help you cope with future stressors, encouraging you to stay motivated and confident in your ability to handle whatever comes your way.

EXPECT THE UNEXPECTED

Professional Dog Trainer and LWDG Group Expert, Samantha Thorncycroft Taylor, taught me the importance of **'expecting the unexpected'** when it comes to dog training. She emphasised that no matter how well-prepared I am, there will always be unexpected setbacks that I will have to navigate.

Learning to expect the unexpected has been a game-changer for me. It's helped me to stay calm when things don't go as planned in my Magic Month Planner, and to keep a positive attitude even when the poop hits the fan. By learning to accept that there will undoubtedly be setbacks, I've been able to develop the confidence I need to push through them when they appear. By accepting this certainty, you too can avoid getting discouraged when things don't go as predicted.

It's important to remember that your growth and development will take time and that progress is far from linear. Stay focused on the bigger picture.

RESILIENCE IN ACTION

Your resilience is one of the most critical components of your training. It allows you to stay focused during chaotic training sessions, alter course to accommodate unexpected dilemmas and bounce back from the colossal f**kups that surprise us some days.

Imagine you're teaching your dog, let's call him Buddy, to come to you when called. You're in your training field and things are going perfectly. Then, out of nowhere, a squirrel (or, let's say, a rabbit) dashes out from a bush. Buddy, being the fun-loving dog he is, forgets everything and chases it. Sh*t!!

So, when you feel like giving up as Buddy dashes off into the distance, don't say, "Well, that's my dog's working days over!" Consider this a golden opportunity. It's like when you're playing a video game and a surprise obstacle pops up. Do you quit? No! You level up your skills.

This is where "proofing" enters the scene. Think of it as levelling up in the training game. Instead of only calling Buddy when things are calm and rabbit-free in future, you learn to add a few distractions into your training. Maybe it's a toy, another dog, some food, or yes, even practising near where those sneaky squirrels and rabbits live. This way, Buddy learns that even when there's super exciting stuff happening around him, he should still listen to you. It's like teaching a kid to focus on homework even when their favourite cartoon is on. It's challenging but totally doable!

Your attitude is key here. Just as you'd cheer on a friend or laugh when you drop your ice cream cone instead of crying, staying positive when training Buddy makes a world of difference. Remember, it's not about being perfect. It's about having fun and learning together. So, the next time Buddy gets distracted, give him a wink, pull up your big girl/boy pants, adjust your strategy, and say, "Challenge accepted!"

WHEN YOUR MOTIVATION IS LOST

One of the most significant hurdles to jump in dog training is dealing with your dwindling motivation. When your motivation starts to slip away, maintaining concentration and commitment towards your training goals can feel like an uphill battle. It can seem like an impossible task and can often make you question why you embarked on this massive expedition into dog training in the first place.

Motivation often disappears when setbacks are encountered. For example, you may spend weeks teaching your dog a new command, only to find they seem to have forgotten it the very next day. Or perhaps, despite your best efforts, your dog just doesn't seem to be making the progress you expected. Moments like these can be disheartening and can seriously dampen your drive to continue training.

Moreover, it's not just about setbacks in training. Life, in general, can sometimes throw a curveball that leaves you feeling demoralised. Personal issues, work-related stress, health problems - like my own experience with the brain tumour, or even a pandemic like COVID, can all chip away at your enthusiasm and focus at doing anything with your four-legged friend. You might find yourself feeling emotionally drained. With your energy reserves so depleted, it feels impossible to bring your 'A' game to your training sessions.

When motivation is lost, even the simplest tasks can seem daunting. You might notice that you're more likely to skip training sessions or you might find yourself going through the motions without truly engaging with your dog. This can create a vicious cycle: the less motivated you are, the less progress you see, which, in turn, further decreases your motivation, weakening your motivation going forward.

It's important to remember that these periods of low motivation are common and almost everyone experiences them at some point. The key is to be conscious of this dip in motivation and take active steps to rekindle that initial spark. Remind yourself of why you decided to train your dog in the first place and remember the joy you feel at the end of a successful session.

Remember, it's okay to have bad days or even bad weeks. Take a step back when you need to recharge. You will have days where your challenges feel almost impossible, they are the days it's important to ask for help or seek advice from others. You may find their new ideas or fresh perspectives make you feel excited to try again. Never be scared to look for the help you need. What matters most is that you don't let these setbacks define your training, but instead, view them as temporary hurdles that you're fully capable of overcoming.

HOW DOUBTING YOURSELF CAN LEAD TO BURNOUT

One of the biggest adversities to your resilience building is experiencing burnout. The persistent self-doubt and the constant questioning of your capabilities can lead to emotional and mental exhaustion.

Life's a bit like baking a cake. Most days, you're adding the right ingredients, following the recipe and everything's mixing just fine. But then, some days, you accidentally dump in a whole bag of salt instead of sugar. Suddenly, your sweet, fluffy cake turns into a salty mess. That's burnout for you!

Burnout sneaks in when you've been pushing yourself too hard for too long. It's the feeling you get when, instead of baking one cake, you've been trying to bake five, all at once, without a break. And not just any cakes, but five-tiered wedding cakes with intricate designs!

This relentless hustle can have you questioning your chef skills. "Am I even good at baking?" or "Maybe I should've just bought a cake from the store." Doubts start piling up like unwashed dishes, leading to mental and emotional exhaustion.

But here's the sweet part: just as every baker has a flopped cake now and then, it's okay to feel burnt out. It doesn't mean you're not a stellar baker; it just means you need a breather.

Remember, resilience in the kitchen (and in life) isn't about never making mistakes; it's about finding ways to make a cake the way you always do, or even better than normal the next time around.

Dog training, like cake baking, can be a demanding task, requiring substantial amounts of time, energy and dedication. Pair this with the constant struggle of self-doubt, and you have a recipe for burnout. The constant worries about whether you're doing enough, or if you're doing it right, can drive you mad. When these doubts start creeping in, they can rob you of your enthusiasm, making training feel like a chore.

Moreover, in your quest to become an expert dog owner and trainer, it's very easy to neglect other areas of your life. Balancing training commitments with work, personal life, and self-care can become an overwhelming juggling act, leaving you feeling stretched thin.

The stress of managing these competing priorities, coupled with self-doubt, can lead to exhaustion. Burnout isn't just about feeling tired; it's a state of chronic physical and emotional tiredness, a loss of motivation, decreased productivity, and feelings of helplessness. In this state, building and maintaining your resilience becomes a formidable task.

So, it's vital to recognise when you're pushing yourself too hard and to take preventive measures to avoid exhaustion. Remember, it's okay, and absolutely necessary, to take breaks when you need them. Breaks offer an opportunity to rest, recharge and regain your strength. It's during these moments of pause that you can gather your thoughts, reassess your approach, eat your lovely cake and return to training with renewed passion and a clearer mind.

Practising self-care is key to avoiding burnout. This could mean setting aside time each day for activities you enjoy outside of dog training, maintaining a healthy diet, getting regular exercise and ensuring you have enough sleep. We will talk about this further in this book.

THE IMPORTANCE OF SELF-COMPASSION

Whether it's in life or dog training, self-compassion plays a pivotal role. With our dogs, it's not uncommon to hit roadblocks that invite unwelcome self-doubt, shaking the confidence we're working hard to establish.

Take my experience with my dog, Ella, for instance. My goal was simple: teach her to walk nicely beside me. But Ella, with her love for the world's wonders, would easily get side-tracked, tugging over-enthusiastically on her slip lead. Progress seemed slower than anticipated. At times, it even felt like we were regressing.

This led to a spiral of self-blame. Thoughts like "I should've mastered this by now" crowded my mind, making me question my abilities. This cloud of negativity not only weighed on me but also affected Ella. It was clear that she could sense my stress, which only added to our problem.

But there was a turning point. Embracing self-compassion was the game-changer. I took a step back and gave myself grace. I focused on the fact that many spaniel owners grapple with heelwork and that it's natural to find some aspects difficult. Instead of focusing on the issues, I celebrated our tiny victories and milestones. By nurturing my own well-being and emotional health, I rediscovered the enthusiasm essential for effective training.

Today, Ella's heelwork has seen remarkable improvement. It might not be textbook perfect, but it's our version of perfect. And to think, we might've missed this journey if I had succumbed to self-doubt. Embracing self-compassion didn't just benefit me – it transformed our training.

A very important part of being kind to yourself is identifying your strengths and accepting areas for improvement. It also means understanding that it's okay to make mistakes and face difficulties - these are normal parts of learning to train a dog.

Another helpful way to be kinder to yourself is changing how you talk to yourself when things get tough. For instance, instead of thinking, "I'm bad at training," you can change that thought to, "I'm still learning, and every mistake helps me get better".

By thinking this way, we can be more understanding and patient with ourselves. This helps us stay strong and keep going, even when training our dogs gets challenging.

WAYS IN WHICH WE CAN IMPROVE

Believing in your ability to develop through adopting an evolving outlook, allows you to approach training problems as opportunities to gain experience and grow, rather than seeing them as impassable roadblocks. This mindset helps you stay motivated.

A growth mindset is a concept introduced by psychologist Carol Dweck after years of research on achievement and success. This idea can fundamentally change the way we approach challenges, setbacks and self-improvement.

There are two primary mindsets we can navigate life with:

Fixed Mindset: People with a fixed mindset think that their abilities, intelligence and talents are static traits. They think they have a certain amount of intelligence and that's that. They might avoid challenges because failures might reflect upon their set level of abilities and make them feel like they're not good enough or that they've been overestimated. They see effort as pointless because they believe that if you can do something, it should come naturally.

Growth Mindset: On the other hand, individuals with a learning mindset believe that abilities and intelligence can be developed with effort, learning and persistence. They embrace challenges, seeing them as opportunities to learn and grow. They are resilient in the face of obstacles and view effort as a necessary pathway to mastery. Failures or setbacks aren't seen as evidence of unintelligence or a lack of talent, but as a catalyst for growth and for stretching existing abilities.

The beauty of a progressive mentality lies in its emphasis on the power of persistence and the learning process. Dweck's research has shown that when people adopt an expandable mindset, they tend to achieve more, not just because they see effort positively, but because they are more resilient in the face of challenges, setbacks and criticism.

Fixed Mindset in Dog Training:

Scenario: You're trying to train your dog, Max, to retrieve a dummy. After several attempts, Max still doesn't get it.

Fixed Mindset Reaction:

- "Max just isn't a retrieve kind of dog."
- "Maybe some dogs are naturally good at retrieving and Max isn't one of them."
- "I'm probably not good at teaching dogs. Perhaps I just don't have the knack for it."
- Avoiding trying to teach Max any new cues in the future, believing that neither Max nor you have the capability to learn and improve.

Growth Mindset Reaction:

- "Maybe I need to approach teaching Max in a different way. Let's try a new technique."
- "Retrieving might be challenging for Max, but with persistence and consistent training, he'll get there."
- "Every dog is different. What works for one might not work for another. I need to understand Max better and tailor the training to his needs."
- Seeking advice or researching different training techniques, accepting that both you and Max are on a learning journey and can improve with time and effort.

If you have a fixed mindset, both your dog's and your abilities are seen as static. If you fail, it's perceived as a limitation of your capabilities. With adaptive thinking, challenges in dog training are seen as opportunities for both your dog and you to learn, adapt and grow. There's a belief that with the right strategies and persistence, improvement is possible.

Cultivating a growth-orientated outlook can lead to increased motivation, better achievement and higher levels of success in various fields. Importantly, it's not just about praising effort for the sake of it but understanding that growth and understanding come with time, dedication and a willingness to learn.

In my interview with Professional Gundog Trainer, Sarah Miles, for the Gundog Journal, she astutely likened dog training to a bucket being filled with layers of sand. Think of each training session as a handful of sand; with every session, the bucket becomes more filled. Similarly, every dog you train adds yet another layer and the beauty is, the more sessions you have and the more dogs you interact with, the quicker your bucket fills and the more proficient you become.

But there's a shortcut to speed up this filling process: learning from others. The members of LWDG actively participate in "Ask Us Anything" coaching sessions. Here, they not only address their own problems but listen to the concerns of fellow members. The group experts then provide solutions, which everyone benefits from. In doing so, members are not just adding their own sand, but they're benefiting from the collective wisdom of the group, rapidly building their layers of knowledge by understanding and assimilating solutions to problems they might not have even encountered yet. This collaborative learning accelerates their journey to becoming seasoned dog trainers. At its core, a forward-thinking attitude embraces the idea that abilities and intelligence can be developed through dedication, effort and learning from experiences, both our own and those of others. We understand that by listening to others, we can accelerate our learning curve, thus filling our buckets faster.

Surrounding yourselves with supportive friends, experienced professional trainers or dog training communities, can encourage and motivate us to keep going. Joining a local dog training club or an online forum can provide valuable resources, advice and camaraderie.

Setting realistic goals is essential for building your motivation and resilience. Establishing achievable goals allows you to track your progress, celebrate your successes and avoid getting discouraged by slow progress. Focusing on teaching one command at a time and celebrating each small victory can help maintain motivation throughout your sessions.

Incorporating these strategies into your dog training approach will help you build the mental toughness needed to overcome any obstacles, stay focused and achieve your goals, ultimately leading to a stronger bond with your dog and a more enjoyable training experience.

CHAPTER SNAPSHOT:

- Recognise the importance of resilience in dog training and commit to developing it.
- Practice self-compassion by being kind and gentle with yourself, reframing negative thoughts and prioritising self-care.
- Expect the unexpected and be adaptable to unforeseen issues.
- Set realistic goals and break down complex tasks into manageable steps.
- Seek support from others, such as friends, trainers and mentors, when facing setbacks.
- Maintain a positive mindset and view problems as opportunities for growth and learning.
- Remember that developing resilience requires constant practice and patience, and it never really ends.

READER EXERCISES

1. Create a list of your 'go-to' coping strategies when facing problems. How can you improve this?
2. Write about a time when you used resilience and overcame a setback or obstacle in your dog training.

FINAL THOUGHTS...

When I first started out as a working dog owner, it quickly became clear to me that resilience isn't just a buzzword — it's the foundation. That's precisely why I'm discussing it right up front in this book. Having faith in myself, in my skills and intuition, has been the cornerstone of the connection I've built with my dogs so far. By building my endurance against those moments of doubt, the second-guessing started to fade. Trust me, the path hasn't always been straightforward, but resilience has been my strength. It's encouraged a flexible perspective, which is crucial when obstacles pop up. And they will. Embracing change, adjusting techniques and staying open to learning has not only cemented my relationship with my dogs but has also been pivotal in not letting me give up and make them both unemployed. Sure, I suspend them sometimes, but we soon get back to work.

CHAPTER 5
WHEN LIFE CHANGES, SO DOES TRAINING

Life, as you know, is a constant flux of changes. Some of these changes are unforeseen, springing on you without any warning, while others are more predictable and planned, like the decision to train a working dog. Regardless of their nature, these changes can influence your lives significantly, often in ways you could never have anticipated.

As a working dog owner, you are poised to experience a broad spectrum of changes. One of these transformations is deciding to train a working dog. This decision, while exciting, can turn your routine upside down. Suddenly, you must adjust your daily schedule, allocate time for training, understand your dog's unique personality and needs and adapt your lifestyle to accommodate this new responsibility.

Such changes can bring about new thoughts, feelings and behaviours within you. The quiet, calm hours you used to enjoy might now be replaced with active training sessions. Your patience might be tested time and time again as your dog learns and makes mistakes. You may even have to face criticism or advice from others, forcing you to rethink your strategies.

Have you ever experienced a significant life-altering event? One that made every day different. Maybe losing a loved one, getting divorced, losing a job, or being diagnosed with an illness?

When I was diagnosed with my first brain tumour in 2010, I required a massive operation and I totally fell apart. The world I once knew was replaced with fear, uncertainty and a fragility I hadn't previously acknowledged. Hospital beds, medical jargon and a symphony of beeping machines became my temporary reality.

A year after my operation, life delivered another gut-wrenching blow; the tumour had begun to regrow. This news was almost more shattering than the initial diagnosis, as it felt like a cruel rewind of a chapter I had painstakingly tried to close. With the regrowth came not only the physical setbacks but a more profound loss; I felt as if I was losing even more fragments of my identity and my spirit, and the essence of who I was seemed to have changed completely.

Time seemed to blend in a series of doctor visits, MRI Scans and sleepless nights, each day heavier than the last. Five hard years passed in this manner, with every echo of hope of finding myself again seeming more distant than ever. But then, a turning point arrived in the most unexpected of forms: working dogs.

Those initial days out with the dogs were more than just steps; they were a journey back to me. The pure, unadulterated joy of a dog hunting, their unconditional love and the simple rhythm of our walks became a therapeutic escape. These moments pulled me away from the overbearing shadows of the hospital and into the sunshine of the present. Their wagging tails, determined focus and the unconditional love they radiated became my anchor in a sea of chaos. They reminded me of the beauty of the now, the importance of small joys and the incredible healing power of nature and companionship.

Those dogs had transformed into a lifeline. They grounded me, gave me a purpose and, crucially, reignited a spark within that I feared I had lost forever. While the journey was far from over, they saved my sanity, teaching me that even in the darkest times, hope and healing can come from the most unexpected sources.

Dogs can be a great source of comfort and support during times of change and my dogs saved me from a very dark place (and still do, daily). They also really helped me cope with the loss of Dad in 2019.

These events I faced have fundamentally changed me and set me on a new path in my life. They have made me question who I was, what I believed in and what I wanted to achieve. I am learning that change, no matter how difficult, can actually lead to incredible amounts of personal growth and development.

Throughout this chapter, I want to help you understand how life-altering events can impact you as an individual and a working dog owner. In addition, I want to provide you with practical advice and strategies for coping with and embracing change.

Being able to adapt to big things will make you far more able to cope with both the minor and major changes you're going to face as you learn and grow as a dog trainer. You will learn practical strategies for adapting to changes in your life and how to approach new struggles with a newfound mindset.

Your development as a dog trainer will always be changing. Life events like having a baby, a change in work hours, or even your dog getting older can affect your dog and the way you train them. It's really important to be flexible and change your methods to deal with new situations. This might seem a bit scary, but by being open to change and being willing to adjust, you can come up with new ways to help you and your dog handle any problems.

Whether you're dealing with a change in your dog's behaviour, getting used to training your dog in a new home or simply trying to keep a regular training schedule, it's important to be adaptable and open to change. By being ready to adjust your approach as needed, you'll be more capable of handling anything that comes your way.

LEARNING FROM CHANGE

Change is a predictable part of life, we might not know who, what, where, when and why, but we damn sure know it's coming. And change affects both us and our dogs.

Positive changes are great; they can lead to excitement, happiness, personal growth and progress, while negative changes can cause huge stress and anxiety. However, regardless of the type of change, it can be difficult to navigate, especially if it is a huge, unexpected transformation - it could be the heartbreaking kind or an opportunity in disguise. To cope with shifts in life, developing and nurturing an adaptable approach is key, so if you skipped the last chapter and its exercises, please do them before reading on.

Life is full of twists and turns that can shake up everything from your daily routine to your emotional state. But you know what? Each change is also an opportunity to strengthen your bond with your dog and build a stronger support network. Say you face a health setback. Your dog can become the pillar that keeps you motivated. Or if you move home, it's a chance to create a fresh routine that benefits you both. So, rather than dreading life's ups and downs, see them as openings for new connections and experiences.

Your personal growth and your approach to change go hand in hand, much like the steps you will teach a dog to retrieve a dummy. They aren't separate; they fit together and help each other, just like the different parts of retrieval training. Think about it this way, when you teach your dog to retrieve it's not just about the dog getting the dummy, this single task is made up of so many different parts. There's the 'sit' part, where your dog learns to stay still until you tell them to do something else. Then there's the 'retrieve' part where your dog learns to come straight back to you when you call them. These different parts, even though they are separate, come together to make up the retrieve task. You cannot always control life, but you can control your thoughts, emotions and responses.

In the same way, personal growth and change work together. Growing as a person can lead to changes by pushing you to try new things and question your old ways of thinking. On the other hand, going through changes can lead to growth by giving you a chance to learn, adjust and get stronger. Growth and change are not separate things. They're closely connected, each one affecting the other, much like the retrieve. By understanding this, we can see change less as scary and more as a chance to grow and learn.

WHY WE RESIST CHANGE AND WHY IT'S NOT COOL

Alright, let's dive right into it - we all know that one person, maybe it's even ourselves, who'd rather stick with the same old, same old than try something new. Whether it's still using a flip phone in an age of smartphones or sticking to your grandmother's recipe despite new and healthier alternatives, we've all been there. But why do we resist change? And why is this resistance more like shooting ourselves in the foot?

First things first, it's human nature. Our brains are wired to favour routine and predictability. Survival required us to stay alive. Fear kept us safe. It was an internal beacon drawing us away from danger. That's why your old, beaten-up couch feels like the best place in the world, even though a new one would probably be much more comfortable. The devil you know is better than the devil you don't, right? But here's the kicker - this hardwired behaviour was handy back when we were dealing with sabretooth tigers and needed the comfort of routine for survival, but today? Not so much.

The world is changing at a breakneck speed. With new technologies, societal shifts and environmental obstacles knocking at our doors, sticking to the "way things have always been done" isn't just old-fashioned, the fear that used to keep you safe is now holding you back and possibly even harming you.

Let's paint a picture. We've all seen it – people clinging onto their old flip phones or archaic desktop computers, while the rest of us have been swept up by the smartphone and laptop revolution. Initially, it didn't seem like much of a biggie. But as time went on and the digital world evolved, their refusal to update became more than just an endearing quirk. It became a hindrance.

With services and resources increasingly moving online, their technological standstill put them at a distinct disadvantage. Apps, video calls, online shopping, instant access to a world of information - all these advantages remained out of reach. It started impacting their ability to participate in everyday digital life.

But here's the real clincher - their resistance has even stopped some from accessing our group trainings or tuning into our inspirational podcasts. Think about that for a moment. By holding onto their old devices, they have effectively blocked themselves from many of the most innovative parts of the world wide web like video calling, apps and so much more. And all because of a reluctance to step outside their comfort zone and embrace the new.

It's not just about missing out on the latest masterclass (although, let's be real, these are important), it's about staying connected, staying relevant and keeping up with the world around us. This is a textbook example of how resisting change can hold us back, cutting us off from new experiences, opportunities and even our own community.

Now, change isn't always comfortable, in fact, it often comes with a good deal of discomfort and uncertainty, but here's the thing, growth and development aren't rooted in comfort. They are born out of embracing the unknown head-on and learning new things.

So, next time you find yourself resisting a change, stop for a moment. Ask yourself why you're resisting. Is it because of fear, comfort, or simple habit? And then, think about what you might gain by embracing the change. You might be surprised to find that the benefits far outweigh your reservations.

Remember, friends, life is change. The only thing that's truly constant is change itself. Let's not fight it. Instead, let's embrace it, grow with it, and see where it takes us because, in the end, it's not the strongest or the smartest who survive - it's those most adaptable to change.

RESISTING CHANGE IN DOG TRAINING

Let's make this relevant to the book. Let's imagine you've been using the same training techniques that your grandpa used on his dogs. They worked back then, so they should work now, right? Well, not quite.

Just like any other field, dog training has evolved massively over the years. What used to be a heavily punishment-based approach has shifted towards more positive reinforcement methods. This change is backed by countless studies showing that positive methods are not only more effective but also foster a stronger bond. But you're sticking to the old ways because, well, they're familiar. And that's where the trouble starts.

By not embracing change in dog training, you're setting yourself and your dog up for some real disappointments. For one, punishment-based methods can create stress and fear in dogs, leading to behaviour problems and even aggressive responses. It's like trying to fix a car with a hammer - sure, you might get some reaction, but it's certainly not the best tool for the job.

Moreover, by sticking to outdated methods, you're missing out on a whole world of improved techniques that can make training easier, more enjoyable and far more effective.

And the fallout doesn't stop with your own pup. If you're sharing these outdated methods with other dog owners, you're perpetuating a cycle of ineffective and potentially harmful training.

Just think about it - wouldn't it be better to be at the forefront, leading the pack, so to speak, with progressive, proven methods that bring joy and success, instead of sticking with the same old, same old?

Embracing advancements in dog training isn't just about getting with the times; it's about being the best owner you can be, because, at the end of the day, our dogs deserve nothing but the best from us. And if that means trading in the old training manual for a new one, then that's a change worth making.

THE "IF" FACTOR IN DOG TRAINING

My dad had a favourite saying that always made me chuckle. Whenever I found myself getting lost in a spiral of 'what ifs', he'd say with a twinkle in his eye, "Jo, if your aunt had a willy, she'd be your uncle." Apart from its usual cheeky dad humour, it carried a profound message about the pointlessness of speculating on variables that simply don't exist.

In dog training, as in life, there's often a temptation to get bogged down in the world of 'ifs'. "If only my dog was more obedient, training would be easier," "If I had started training earlier, my dog would behave better," "If my dog was a different breed, things would be different,"... and so on. But here's the thing: "if" doesn't change the present reality. It only diverts our attention away from actionable steps and solutions.

Continuously pondering hypothetical scenarios won't alter your dog's behaviour or enhance your training techniques. It only delays actual progress. Instead of dwelling on the "ifs" that could've, would've or should've been, it's more productive to focus on the "now". What can you do in the present moment, given all the realities and constraints? How can you adjust and adapt to ensure you both are getting the most out of your training sessions?

Don't get me wrong; reflection is essential. It helps us understand our past mistakes and ensure we don't repeat them. However, overindulging in the world of "ifs" can be paralysing. It's a bit like trying to drive forward while only looking in the rearview mirror.

HOW DOGS CAN HELP YOU THROUGH CHANGE

Like you, dogs thrive on routine. They are creatures of habit, finding comfort in familiar patterns and schedules. They wake up roughly at the same time each day, look forward to their walks, meals and training, and settle down to sleep when night falls. By sticking to a consistent care and training routine, you not only meet their needs but also establish a rhythm that can be reassuring for you too.

The beauty of this routine is that it goes beyond the basic tasks of feeding or walking your dog. It extends into the training exercises you engage in with your dog, the daily cuddle sessions, the weekly trips to the park or the pet store and even the occasional visit to the vet. These activities form a pattern, a structure to your days, giving both you and your dog a routine to rely on.

During changes in life, when everything seems to be in flux, this routine can be a source of comfort. When your job is stressing you out, when you're moving to a new house, or when a relationship ends, the routine with your dog can provide a touch of normality, a reminder that not everything in your life is changing.

The unwavering affection and companionship of your dog can help ease feelings of loneliness or uncertainty that often accompany change. Their enthusiasm for simple routines, their joy in seeing you at the end of the day, and their undemanding companionship can provide a sense of grounding, reinforcing the truthful thought that despite the upheaval, some things remain the same. Your dog offers you a lifeline during times of change. Through their need for you to continue some form of routine, they provide a sense of stability that can help you cope with the roadblocks that you face elsewhere.

Let's talk about something magical - the therapeutic power of your dog. While training sessions with your dog can vary between great and gruesome, you might be surprised to learn about the health benefits that just being around them can provide.

Did you know that dogs are natural stressbusters? Studies have shown that simply spending time with your dog can significantly decrease cortisol levels - the hormone associated with stress. That's right, your dog might be providing you with stress relief without you even knowing it!

But there's more to this tale. The act of petting a dog, whether it's a lazy stroke on a Sunday afternoon, or a quick pat as you dash out the door, triggers the release of oxytocin in your body. Oxytocin is often referred to as the "bonding hormone" or the "love hormone", playing a key role in building social connections and promoting relaxation.

So, what does this all mean? Well, it means that your dog isn’t just reducing stress and anxiety but is also enhancing your relationship with them, promoting a sense of calm and relaxation, just by being around you. Now, isn't that something? So, the next time you're feeling stressed or anxious, remember you've got a furry little therapist wagging their tail right by your side.

Your dog also provides you with unconditional love and support, which can be especially valuable during times of change. Dogs don't judge you or hold grudges, and they are always there to offer a comforting presence. This can be especially helpful during times of transition when you may be feeling vulnerable or uncertain.

My Spaniels aren't just my pets; they're my lifeline. As I face my neurological challenges, particularly my tumours, their presence has been so comforting. They might not understand the complexities of my condition, but every wag, every gentle gaze, every time they sit beside me, they help me to keep going.

My dogs remain one of my strongest pillars of support. With every letter that arrives from my consultant, with every MRI scan I attend, they are there, grounding me, reminding me of the joys in life amidst the trials. Without them, I question if I'd be the person I am today, facing my conditions with the strength and grace needed.

EMBRACING CHANGE

Whether it's changes in your dog's behaviour, changes in your personal life, or changes in your training methods, you will face many new uncertainties.

And embracing change can be a good thing. It might feel scary at first, but it can also be an opportunity for you to find the confidence and reliance to further your development. In addition, when you embrace change, you're opening yourself up to new experiences, knowledge and ways of thinking about yourself and the world around you.

By embracing change, you develop a growth mindset. This means that instead of seeing issues as impossible obstacles, you see them as chances to learn and grow. As a result, you become more adaptable, more resilient, and more open to new ideas and perspectives.

In contrast, someone with a fixed mindset may view change as a threat to their established routines or beliefs and struggle to adapt to new circumstances. As a result, they may be more likely to give up when faced with difficulty or see setbacks as evidence of their inherent limitations rather than as opportunities for development.

People with a fixed mindset tend to believe that their abilities are fixed and unchangeable. They think that they either have natural talent or they don't and that there's little they can do to improve their skills or abilities.

This can be a problem when it comes to training dogs because successful training requires persistence, adaptability and a willingness to learn from mistakes. When you have a fixed mindset, you're less likely to be open to new ideas or to try new things. You might give up easily when things don't go according to plan or become frustrated when your dog isn't progressing as quickly as you'd like.

Your mindset and adaptability greatly impact your success as a dog trainer. By constantly working on developing an advancement mentality and embracing change as an opportunity for growth, you'll be more likely to achieve your training goals and build an effective partnership with your dog. In addition, change can also help you to develop greater self-awareness. When you step outside your comfort zone and try new things, you better understand your strengths, weaknesses and limitations. This can help you make better decisions, set more meaningful goals and, ultimately, achieve greater success and fulfilment. Instead of seeing change as a threat or a hindrance, you can view it as an opportunity to improve.

Of course, accepting change can be challenging. It can be uncomfortable, and it requires you to take risks and try new things. But the rewards are worth it. By stepping outside your comfort zone, you can develop new skills, expand your knowledge, and build a stronger, more effective partnership with your dog.

BALANCING YOUR CORE BELIEFS WITH DOG OWNERSHIP

Bringing a dog into your life brings about inevitable changes and it's key for you, as a dog owner, to match your core values with these shifts and the responsibilities they bring. Distinguishing and understanding your values - the principles that guide your life - involves a thorough reflection on what truly matters to you, what lifestyle you aspire to and what goals you're aiming for.

Understanding these values and using them in your relationship with your dog is important. If, for example, you highly value kindness and care, this will naturally translate into ensuring your dog's well-being. If responsibility is a key principle for you, it might mean you're more inclined to dedicate time and effort to properly training your dog to be well-behaved.

My teenage daughter, Meg, has always been surrounded by the comforting presence of dogs, their boundless love and loyalty framing her childhood. Yet recently, having Goose, her very own poodle cross pup named after her unwavering love for the iconic movie "Top Gun", has been an enlightening journey of its own. Now, three weeks into this new chapter, the Instagram-perfect fantasies she might have had of puppy ownership are continually replaced by real-life moments. The demanding 5 am wake-up calls, relentless toilet training, and the need for establishing house manners have made Meg dig deep within herself. She's had to truly embrace her core values: caring, compassion, understanding and patience. As a family, we've frequently reminded her, especially during the tougher times, "He's just a baby, Meg. It's not personal." These moments of gentle counsel have been influential in shaping their new bond, grounding her expectations and encouraging growth through change for both Meg and Goose.

Here's why this awareness is vital for you as an owner and a trainer to draw on your internal values: It's the compass that will guide you through the unexpected storms of change that dog ownership can bring.

Diving deep into your values is about understanding the very fabric of your decisions and actions. It forces you to consider the type of owner you want to be and how you plan to interact with your dog. Gaining clarity on these aspects can help you understand the motivations behind your decisions and the way your values inform your dog ownership style.

If you value honesty, this might prompt you to be transparent about your dog's needs and your capabilities to meet them, you may realise you need to ask for help. If you're someone who values personal growth, dog ownership could be viewed as an opportunity to learn and grow, constantly seeking new knowledge and skills to enhance your ability to care for your pet.

Furthermore, understanding your values provides a spotlight on areas where you might need to adjust your approach to dog care. If you value a balanced life, you might need to reconfigure your routine to ensure both you and your dog's needs are met. If you love adventure, finding ways to include your dog in your explorations might be necessary. A change in your living situation or a shift in your financial standing could significantly affect your routine or resources. But armed with a clear understanding of your values, you can navigate these changes effectively, still ensuring your dog's needs are met. This could involve developing a new routine that provides your dog with enough exercise and social interaction or reworking your budget to provide your pet with necessary healthcare.

And why is this important? Because it shapes the very core of your dog ownership. Aligning your values with your actions not only leads to a more fulfilling experience for you, but it also contributes to a happier and healthier life for your dog. It allows you to steer the inevitable hurdles with confidence, cultivating a balanced and rewarding partnership with your dog.

Your values can also spotlight where adjustments are needed. If you're someone who gets easily frustrated, consider working in shorter training sessions with a young dog and devise a "time-out" plan for yourself to prevent feelings of overwhelm. If you value a balanced life - something many of us aspire to, yet in practice, can be quite elusive - but find all your spare time consumed by training, you might decide to carve out time for other interests.

LIFE BEYOND DOG TRAINING

When you're passionate about something - like dog training - it's all too easy for it to consume every spare moment. Suddenly, you look up and realise that your life has become singularly focused.

That's when it's necessary to step back and reassess. The pursuit of a balanced life often means making time for various interests and passions, not just one. This is a lesson I've had to learn myself.

Don't get me wrong, I adore both my work with the LWDG and training my gundogs. There's a tremendous thrill in watching a dog you've trained yourself respond to your cues. But it's also important to remember that we are multifaceted beings with diverse interests and needs.

Recently I've started to learn sugar craft and piano playing. The precise attention to detail and artistic creativity of sugar craft provide a different kind of satisfaction, a gentle contrast to the energetic focus of gundog training. I find the activity meditative, a quiet space where I can let my mind wander as my hands make delicate sugar flowers and intricate buttercream designs.

Piano playing, on the other hand, engages a different part of my brain. It's about rhythm, timing and focus- not unlike dog training, in some ways, but applied in a completely different context. The melodies and harmonies offer an emotional outlet and serve as a pleasant distraction, pulling me away from the training ground, or the computer, and into a world of music.

These hobbies don't just offer respite, but they also enrich my life, bringing in diversity and balance. It's like opening windows in different corners of my mind, letting in fresh air, and ensuring all parts of me are nurtured, not just the "Founder" or "gundog trainer".

Striving for a balanced life might mean adjusting your routine to incorporate more of your interests. Whether it's picking up a new hobby, devoting more time to an old one, or simply setting aside time for quiet reflection, it's about making space for more than just one aspect of your life. And trust me, not only will you feel more satisfied, but your gundog training might just benefit from your broader perspective and rejuvenated spirit.

CHANGES IN YOUR DOG TRAINING JOURNEY

Your training with your dog will be ever-evolving. As your dog grows and develops, their needs will change, and you'll need to adapt your training methods accordingly. Similarly, changes in your circumstances may require you to adjust your training approach. When our lives are in flux, it can be challenging to maintain the consistency needed in our training, which will lead to frustration and setbacks.

Recently, we moved to a new house, and it was a big change for me and for our dogs. It took a lot of time and energy to get used to our new place. We had to unpack, set up the new house and learn about our new area. This took up so much of my time that I couldn't spend as much time with my dogs as I wanted.

Before we moved, I had a regular routine for myself and my dogs. We knew roughly when it was time for walks, training, and rest. But after moving, all of that changed. I was so busy that it was hard to keep up with our normal schedule. I could tell this was hard for my dogs too.

My dogs were upset by the move. The new house was very different for them. They seemed a bit worried and acted differently, like not eating at their normal times and seeming restless. There is a smaller garden, access to a country park has gone and we are close to a busy road.

Moving was a big adjustment, but it showed me how important routine and familiar places are to us. When big changes happen, it's important to recognise them and adjust as best as we can. This helps keep our dogs, and ourselves, happy and balanced. As we have all gotten more used to our new home, we now have a new 'normal'. The new sound of the garage door going up tells Rex I'm about to get his meals, The sound of the door chime tells them if someone is coming in or out of our house, the coffee machine tells them the house is waking up each morning and the sound of the road isn't heard by any of us anymore.

CHANGES IN YOUR DOG'S BEHAVIOUR

Sometimes, it's not life circumstances that change, but your dog's behaviour. Changes in a dog's behaviour can stem from numerous causes, both subtle and pronounced. Health issues, for instance, can prompt shifts in behaviour; a dog in pain or discomfort might become aggressive or lethargic. Dental problems might lead a dog to avoid food. Older dogs might exhibit signs of vision or hearing loss, causing disorientation. As they age, cognitive decline becomes another factor, leading to confusion or forgetfulness. Emotional traumas, such as a negative encounter or significant household changes, like the death of a loved one, can profoundly influence actions, leading to anxiety or depression. Even simple environmental alterations, like moving homes or shifting furniture, can unsettle a dog. Inadequate training or socialisation, often noticeable in dogs not properly introduced to various experiences as puppies, can result in anxiety. Diet plays a role too; certain foods or additives might trigger hyperactivity or mood swings, and reproductive hormones in dogs that aren't spayed or neutered can induce hormone-driven deeds. A lack of mental stimulation and exercise can breed frustration, manifesting in unwanted activities like excessive barking or destruction. Fears and phobias, whether from past traumas or developing naturally, can lead to noticeable behavioural shifts. In essence, any behavioural change in a dog signals a need for attention and possibly intervention, be it through a vet's guidance or consultation with a professional dog trainer.

These changes can require some major adjustments on your part, especially when it comes to your training approach. It's not always easy - in fact, it can feel like you're suddenly facing a daunting uphill climb. In these cases, your old methods of training may no longer be effective. You might find yourself needing to learn new techniques or seeking advice from a professional dog trainer or vet. Adolescence kicking in, without a doubt, causes worry for many of our members.

This shift in your dog's behaviour might feel frustrating and overwhelming, however, it's important to remember that just like humans, dogs go through changes too. It's all part of their development and while it's challenging, it also presents an opportunity for you to learn and grow along with them.

Think of it like adjusting the sails on a boat when the wind changes direction. It's about learning how to work with the wind change rather than against it. By staying open to change you can find a way to navigate these shifts in behaviour. It might take time and patience, but with persistence, you'll be able to overcome, or if it's a permanent change, at the least manage them. Our oldest daughter Charlotte's experience with her agility dog, Lady, serves as a moving example of this principle in action. Lady, despite her young age and youthful enthusiasm, started attending physio sessions for problems with her back. After many months, lots of improvement, but still not enough, Charlotte and the physiotherapist made the tough decision to retire Lady from agility, acknowledging that the sport was exacerbating her back issues. While this could have been a disheartening moment for many, Charlotte showed resilience and adaptability. Instead of dwelling on the setback, she sought out alternative activities that Lady could engage in, activities that wouldn't strain her back but would still keep her active and joyful. Just as one might adjust sails to changing winds, Charlotte has adapted to Lady's needs, proving that with a positive outlook and a bit of creativity, one can find a way forward even after unexpected changes in course.

One of the keys to successfully working through changes in your dog training experience is to remain open to new ideas and approaches. Seek advice and support from other working dog owners, attend training and workshops and experiment with new techniques and methods. Training a dog during times of change requires patience, flexibility and adaptability. Rather than striving for perfection, focus on small steps of progress and celebrate the littlest wins. Be open to entirely adjusting your training methods to fit your current situation, and don't be afraid to ask for help if you need it.

Following a training session, your dog will be coming home with you. What happens on the training field should remain there. Holding onto frustrations and bringing them into your home can create an atmosphere of tension. Dogs, with their keen sense of emotion, can pick up on this, potentially affecting their well-being and your bond. It's essential to separate the challenges faced during training from the daily interactions at home. Just as we don't want our day's worries following us home, we shouldn't let a tough training session colour our entire day with our dog. Learn to release and reset, ensuring that your home remains a place of calm. Of course, if the issue is within the home, this will need further attention and possibly a different approach. Home is the primary environment where you and your dog bond and interact daily. If behavioural or training challenges persist in this space, it might be beneficial to seek professional guidance or employ specific in-home strategies to address the root cause. Remember, a harmonious home is foundational for both you and your dog's overall well-being, and promoting a peaceful environment is worth the additional effort.

THE IMPORTANCE OF BEING IN THE RIGHT STATE OF MIND WHEN TRAINING YOUR DOG

During times of change, it's also essential to prioritise self-care and recognise your own limits. Training a dog can be a time-consuming and emotionally draining process, and it's important to take breaks when needed and address your mental and physical health. Be conscious of the impact that changes in your own life can have on your dog's training and think about how to be proactive in addressing these issues.

As a dog trainer, it's important to acknowledge the impact that our state of mind can have on our dogs when we are training. When you're angry, frustrated or stressed, your dog is likely to pick up on these emotions and respond in kind. This can lead to confusion and miscommunication, which can set back your training progress.

My dad used to tell me a story about knowing as an owner when it's best to leave the dog alone and not to train. The tale goes that a man was so angry with his wife that he went out to train and took his anger out on their dog by training it harshly. The dog learned the lesson, but never trusted the man again.

This tale highlights the importance of being in the right state of mind when training your dog. When you are in a negative emotional state, especially when you face a huge change, you're more likely to transfer those negative emotions to your dogs, leading to undesirable behaviours and setbacks in training.

As I write this, at 6am in the morning, Meg's pup lays at my feet. I can tell the early 5am toilet trips to the garden during school holidays are hard, so now and then, I step in and help. Better she's well slept and can cope with him for the rest of the day than I force her up and then both suffer emotionally. The same goes if you really are not in the right place to train the dog. One session missed is better than a bond broken. Perhaps you're dealing with personal issues or you're simply feeling overwhelmed. During such times, it might be best to take a step back and give both yourself and your dog a break. Remember, training should be a positive and enjoyable experience for both of you. If you're not feeling up to it, it's okay to pause and resume when you're feeling better.

Approach dog training with a clear, calm and positive mindset. Take time to centre yourself before starting a training session and focus on clearly communicating with your dog. If you can't find it in yourself to do this, forgive yourself and knock the training on the head. Better to take the dog for a peaceful walk or, if needed, go by yourself, rather than try to train and cause even more anguish to your already frayed emotions.

REDISCOVERING PURPOSE AND MOTIVATION

Sometimes, we can feel incredibly deflated with our dog training and it's important we find the purpose and motivation to keep moving forward. You can adapt to changes with your dog without losing motivation by maintaining a positive outlook. This is crucial, particularly when events don't unfold as you had envisioned. It's natural to feel disheartened in these situations, but holding onto a positive and hopeful attitude can serve as a catalyst in persevering through your setbacks.

Always be on the lookout for innovative thoughts or methods in your approach to training. Having the courage to venture out of your comfort zone can provide you with fresh perspectives and possibilities. Keep conscious of the fact that what worked in the past might not work in the present or future, so be willing to adapt your training methods to meet your dog.

However, while seeking new methods and strategies, be cautious of the 'shiny object syndrome'. This is the tendency to jump from one new idea or method to another, always chasing the next 'big thing' without fully committing to or mastering any particular approach. It's essential to differentiate between genuinely innovative methods that can enhance your training and those that simply distract from consistent, effective techniques. Diversifying your tactics is valuable, but it's equally vital to ensure consistency and avoid overwhelming both yourself and your dog with too many changes in a short period.

Stay patient. Training a dog takes time and patience. Be prepared to invest the time and effort required to achieve your goals and be patient with yourself and your dog. Don't hesitate to ask for help when needed. Reading books, investing in online courses, listening to podcasts, joining a training group or seeking advice from a professional trainer can be great ways to adapt your training skills.

Learn from your mistakes when things don't go according to plan. Examine what went wrong and consider how you can do things differently in the future. Training a dog is a long process and the path isn't always straightforward, but by staying open-minded, positive and flexible, you'll be more likely to achieve your goals.

MOVING FORWARD

You are sure to face various twists and turns during your training sessions. Welcoming change and keeping an open mind to new ideas and tactics, allows you to adjust and progress with your dogs, fostering a more robust and effective partnership. Rather than fearing or battling change, regard it as a chance to learn and evolve.

Remember, it's perfectly fine to stumble, after all, it's human, right? Stumbling is a normal part of learning. If we tackle problems with a mindset focused and eager to learn and adapt, we can achieve lasting success.

CHAPTER SNAPSHOT:

- Acknowledge that change is a natural part of life and can have both positive and negative impacts.
- Understand how unexpected events and changes can impact you as an individual and a working dog owner.
- Recognise the importance of adapting to new circumstances that arise in your training with your dog.
- Adapt to changes with your dog by being open-minded, flexible, patient, seeking support and learning from mistakes.
- Remember that setbacks are a natural part of learning and approach issues with a learning mindset to achieve long-term success.

READER EXERCISES

1. Make a list of your values and beliefs and identify how they align with your responsibilities as a dog owner.
2. Write a letter to your future self, exploring your vision for your dog ownership adventure. Write it starting with the following sentence – 'Regardless of the changes life is going to throw at us, my dog and I will…'

FINAL THOUGHTS...

I know personally how intimidating change can be. Yet, I've also come to see it as a profound chance for growth. When you approach change with a flexible mindset and an eagerness to grow, you'll find yourself better prepared for the challenges ahead. And trust me, it's alright to stumble along the way. We all do. With a touch of patience, a dash of persistence, and a commitment to learning, I believe you'll not only reach your goals but also foster a deep and rewarding bond with your dog.

CHAPTER 6
OVER-CRITICISM

"Over-criticism" is a word in the English dictionary. It is defined as excessive or unjustified criticism, often to the point of discouraging or demotivating someone or something. Another word for our over-criticism could be "hyper-criticism," and it's something I see daily in our community of women, a consumed focus on the smallest of details being perceived as incorrect.

Many of you can be WAY too hard on yourselves and your dogs. You notice every small mistake, and sometimes, you focus almost obsessively on these tiny details. You are overly harsh or picky about things that aren't perfect, and this demoralising habit isn't helpful, especially when you're at the start of your development. When you focus too much on little mistakes, you can forget to notice all the things that are going well. It can make your dog training seem like no fun and more like hard work.

It's important to remember that your dog, like you, isn't perfect. They have their own personalities and sometimes they have off days. They may not always get commands right or respond quickly enough, but that doesn't mean you're failing as a trainer. It's all part of the process.

Your dog, as already discussed, can tell when you're upset or frustrated, even if they don't understand your words. They can pick up on your feelings, and if you're often unhappy, it can make them feel stressed. This can make training harder than it needs to be. Constant self/dog criticism is a sure-fire way of them getting worried.

So, what can you do about it? One of the best things you can do is change your way of thinking. It's not easy, but it is, without doubt, doable. Instead of focusing on every small mistake, you must be patient. Allow yourself time to get to grips with the training criteria at hand. Constantly celebrate the small wins. After all, training your dogs isn't just about teaching them commands. It's about building a strong partnership with them. Over-criticism is a common pitfall in dog training that can have severe negative consequences. It's so important to recognise the dangers, as it can hugely damage your dog's progress and hinder your success.

IT'S THE DOGS FAULT! NO, IT'S MINE!

Constantly criticising your dog for their mistakes and shortcomings can make them anxious, stressed and fearful, which can ultimately harm their learning and development. Dogs, without doubt, respond better to positive reinforcement, and if they are continuously criticised, they may start to doubt their abilities and become less willing to learn. And you do too.

Whilst dogs may not understand the specific words used, they can certainly pick up on your tone and behaviour. Dogs are incredibly intuitive animals, detecting negative emotions in their owners, such as frustration, anger and disappointment. These negative emotions can massively influence your dog. It's fundamental to maintain a positive and encouraging attitude during sessions, even if your dog isn't getting it right away.

Over-criticising yourself as a trainer can be equally damaging. Over-criticising yourself as a trainer can be equally damaging. I wrote that twice on purpose so you take this point in. It's that important.

Making mistakes is inevitable, and it's important to avoid negative self-talk. Instead to be kind to yourself. If you are constantly criticising yourself, you will end up feeling incredibly inadequate and become unmotivated to continue, which ultimately affects progress. In essence, the approach you take toward your dog's learning journey mirrors the approach you take toward your own growth as a trainer. Just as patience, encouragement and understanding are vital components of nurturing your dog's progress, extending the same compassion and patience to yourself is essential for maintaining your enthusiasm. In the next sections, we'll talk about some ways to stop being so hard on yourself and your dog. You'll learn how to be more patient and understanding, which can make training a better experience for both of you.

THE PITFALLS OF NEGATIVE LABELLING

The words we use to describe ourselves and our dogs can have a powerful impact. Labelling our dogs or ourselves based on character traits rather than actions can lead us down a harmful path. For instance, calling your dog "stubborn" or "useless" might create unhelpful feelings. Similarly, if you label yourself as "clumsy" or "thick," you're also setting a damaging narrative about your own abilities. This form of criticism can seriously hurt you and your working dog, who needs to trust in your leadership to do their job effectively.

Instead of saying that your dog is stubborn, consider what's causing the behaviour you're observing. Could it be that your dog doesn't fully understand your command? Or perhaps there's something in the environment that's making your dog uncomfortable or distracted?

Similarly, before labelling yourself as thick, take a moment to reflect on your actions. Are you providing clear, consistent instructions? Are you setting realistic expectations for both you and your dog? Could you benefit from additional training or resources to improve your skills?

Using more specific, behaviour-based language can help you address the root cause of any issues, leading to more helpful solutions. This shift in language can also improve your mindset, encouraging a more constructive approach to struggles. By believing in your ability and your dog's ability to grow and improve, you can foster the problem-solving growth mindset that I keep banging on about.

SETTING REALISTIC EXPECTATIONS IN DOG TRAINING

Setting realistic expectations is a fundamental aspect of dog training. It's essential to have a clear understanding of what you and your dog are capable of and to set goals that are achievable. Setting unrealistic goals leads to such frustration and disappointment. I've used the word goal up until now as it's a term most of us use or are used to hearing and reading about. However, I think setting goals can actually cause huge problems because you see these goals as hard lines drawn in the sand that you either reach or don't. This hard fast line applies huge worry, especially if we feel we failed.

I no longer set goals but intentions.

I find setting intentions can be a far more effective approach than setting firm goals. These intentions set my direction but don't pressure me in a negative way. I'm always working towards my intention.

Goals tend to have specific criteria to achieve, which can create pressure and lead to over-criticism if they are not met. Intentions, on the other hand, are broader and focus on the desired outcome rather than the specific criteria. This approach can create a more relaxed and positive training environment, as it allows for flexibility. It encourages the trainer to focus on the progress and development of the dog rather than meeting specific goals. By setting intentions, you can still have a clear idea of what you want to achieve, while also allowing room for the individuality of each dog and their unique learning pace.

Set expectations for your dog that incorporate you thinking about and understanding your dog's breed, age and personality. For example, some breeds are more naturally inclined towards specific tasks, such as retrieving or hunting. Similarly, older dogs may take longer to learn new skills than younger ones, and some dogs may be more confident or assertive than others. By understanding these factors, you can set intentions that are achievable and tailored to your dog's current abilities.

TRAIN THE DOG IN FRONT OF YOU

Dogs, much like humans, are unique individuals, each with their own learning pace and style. Just as some children might pick up maths faster than reading, or vice versa, dogs too have areas where they excel and others where they might need a bit more practice and patience.

One dog might quickly grasp the concept of 'sit' or 'stay', while another might take a little longer to understand and follow these commands. Some dogs might be naturals at hunting, while others may need extra encouragement and repetition to understand the task. And just as humans can have good days and bad days, so too can our dogs. Some days, they may seem to pick up new tasks effortlessly, while on others, they might struggle with commands they've previously mastered.

The key is to recognise and respect your dog's unique learning pace. Pushing them too hard or expecting them to progress at the same speed as another dog can lead to frustration for both of you. On the LWDG podcast 'Found It, Fetched It', there's a fabulous podcast called, The Working Dog Training Age Race. Feedback from it is incredible and if you can, I would add it to your "must listen" list.

While dogs often hold a cherished place in our homes, akin to family members, the urgency to train them quickly sometimes overshadows our approach. Unlike with horses, where we allow longer training periods due to their physical requirements, dogs often face accelerated training schedules. However, both animals, intelligent in their own right, deserve, in my opinion, a similar amount of patient training.

Training a dog isn't a sprint to the finish; there's no definitive endpoint where you can claim victory. By treating it as a continuous journey rather than a race, you're more likely to forge an environment conducive to learning. Benefits of a gradual training process include:

- Avoiding confusion and preventing overwhelming the dog.
- Cultivating a strong foundation of trust and open communication.
- Making the learning process enjoyable for the dog, turning it into a shared adventure.

Consider your dog's age, breed and temperament when setting all training intentions. Puppies and younger dogs may have shorter attention spans and require shorter, more frequent training sessions. Certain breeds may be more inclined towards specific tasks or commands based on their history and genetics. And, of course, each dog's unique personality can greatly influence their learning style and pace.

Another key aspect of setting realistic expectations is understanding your own limitations as a trainer. It's important to recognise that you may not have all the skills, knowledge or resources necessary to achieve your desired goal.

SETTING REALISTIC EXPECTATIONS FOR YOURSELF

As an owner, when setting intentions, it's important to have a clear understanding of what you want to achieve. This involves identifying your strengths and weaknesses and setting realistic expectations for your progress. For example, if you are new to dog training, it may be unrealistic to expect to master complex skills quickly. Instead, setting intentions to focus on building a strong foundation of basic skills can be a more achievable and realistic approach.

It's also essential to focus on the learning pathway rather than the outcome. Learning new skills can be challenging and requires lots of dedication. Focusing on the process can help you stay motivated and positive, even if you encounter setbacks or difficulties. Being patient can help you avoid over-criticism and self-doubt. Three steps of heelwork should be celebrated as much as a fifty-metre recall.

Appreciating your dog's progress, regardless of its size in relation to progression, plays a pivotal role in effective dog training. When you take note of even the smallest improvements in your dog's behaviour or learning, you are encouraging them in a way that's both supportive and motivating. This sort of reinforcement, especially when coupled with rewards that your dog enjoys, can significantly boost their confidence and motivation to learn. They learn quickly that working with you as a team is beneficial to them. In a nutshell, it transforms the training experience into an enjoyable activity rather than a chore.

Progress will never be along a straight path. There will be bumps along the road, setbacks and mistakes. Instead of viewing these as failures, see them as the opportunities for growth they are. There is so much we can learn from setbacks. Acknowledging and celebrating improvement helps you build a deep library of resilience to use in the face of setbacks. When your dog realises that its effort leads to reward, they're likely to be more persistent. This approach can foster a 'can-do' attitude in your dog, making the training process more effective and enjoyable for both of you.

When you experience a setback in your dog training, take it as an opportunity to assess your strategies and methods. Each setback can provide clues about what works and what doesn't for your particular dog. Maybe your commands aren't clear enough, or perhaps your dog responds better to different forms of motivation. These insights are incredibly valuable and can help guide your future training efforts.

Whilst this book is not about dog training per se (I leave that to our fabulous group experts), what I will say is it's important to avoid allowing mistakes to derail your progress.

Assessing a mistake in dog training is not about beating yourself up mentally; it's about observing and learning from the situation. What was the environment like? What were you thinking? How did this affect your emotions and response? How did this affect the outcome? What about all of these from your dog's perspective? Carry out a review but not an assessment. This isn't a pass/failure or good/bad judgement. Rather than dwelling on the mistake, identify the cause and adjust your training approach if necessary. This involves a constructive and analytical approach, focused on learning and growth rather than negative self-talk and over-criticism.

THE BURDEN OF GUILT: OVERCOMING OVER-CRITICISM

Over-criticism often leads to a huge sense of guilt. Guilt can manifest itself in a variety of ways. You might feel guilty if you're not able to spend as much time as you'd like training your dog, or if your training sessions don't go as planned, or if you have not yet mastered the skills you need to train the command. You might even feel guilty when comparing your progress to others. Guilt can be debilitating. It can cloud your judgment, hinder your progress and strain your relationship with your dog.

Feeling guilty often happens when you're too hard on yourself. It can really get in the way when you're trying to train, and it can massively weigh you down. Guilt can make it hard for you to think clearly. It's important to remember that everyone makes mistakes, and your path to being a great dog trainer is going to be different from anyone else's. Think about when you were learning to ride a bike or play a musical instrument. You didn't just hop on the bike and ride flawlessly or play a tune perfectly the first time, right? There were plenty of falls, wrong notes and do-overs. Yet, you didn't let those initial failures deter you from learning. You persevered, learning from each misstep. The same applies to dog training.

Try not to compare yourself with others. Just as every dog is different, so is every dog owner. What works for one pair might not work for you and your dog. Instead, focus on the progress you and your dog are making together. It's like climbing a ladder; even if you're on the first or second rung, you're still higher than when you were on the ground. Most importantly, let go of the guilt. Nothing productive has ever come from it. Being too hard on yourself only makes you feel stressed and worried, which doesn't help when you're trying to train your dog. Instead, treat yourself kindly. Understand that you're doing your best and appreciate the effort you're putting in. Getting over the guilt from being too hard on yourself is about being positive and forgiving. By doing this, you make training your dog a healthier activity for both of you.

IMPROVING YOUR PATIENCE

Improving patience is a key factor in reducing over-criticism because it allows you to manage expectations and to better understand the learning process for both you and your dog. It can take lots of practice, but there are a few things you can do to improve your patience as a handler. From the outset, it's important to practice mindfulness and be present in the moment during training sessions. This means intentionally focusing on your dog's behaviour and responses and being aware of your own emotions and reactions.

Mindfulness is the practice of bringing full, non-judgmental attention to what's happening in the present moment. This can be extremely helpful in reducing self/dog condemnation for several reasons. Mindfulness keeps you focused on the present moment, rather than getting caught up in past training mistakes or worrying about future progress. This can help you and your dog stay fully absorbed in each training session and prevent you from criticising your dog based on past behaviours, even the ones that happened thirty seconds ago. Practising mindfulness can help to reduce stress and anxiety, which can ultimately improve your results.

By being mindful, you become a better observer of your dog's behaviour, body language and signals. This understanding can help you better tailor your training methods to your dog's individual needs.

Mindfulness also helps with self-regulation, meaning it can help you manage your own emotions and reactions during training sessions. This is where the E-T-e-R-O^2 framework needs to be addressed. Mindfulness can help you stay patient, reducing the likelihood of responding inappropriately.

One of the key aspects of mindfulness is adopting a completely non-judgmental attitude. This means accepting what's happening in the moment without labelling it as "good" or "bad". This can help you avoid labelling or criticising your dog's behaviour and instead see each moment as an opportunity for learning and growth.

Consider a scenario where your dog suddenly barks at a passing cyclist during your walk. A typical reaction might be frustration, thinking "My dog is behaving badly" or "This shouldn't be happening". However, with a mindful, non-judgmental approach, you would acknowledge the event without immediate criticism: "My dog is reacting to the cyclist." This perspective shift allows you to calmly assess the situation, perhaps spotting that your dog might have been startled, curious or simply alerting you. By reframing the event as a learning opportunity, you can then choose to train your dog on how to better react to cyclists in the future, turning a potentially stressful situation into a productive training session.

IF I AM THE PROBLEM, I AM ALSO THE SOLUTION

In the world of training dogs, there may be many moments of self-doubt and uncertainty, particularly for women who lack confidence in their abilities. However, in the face of these challenges, an empowering mantra takes centre stage:

"If I am the problem, I am also the solution."

This powerful statement reminds you that you can overcome the setbacks you have created in training your dog. By acknowledging your role in both the problem and the solution, you inspire yourself to grow. By embracing this mantra in a non-judgemental way as part of your mindfulness, you take control of your progress, gain self-assurance and develop the competence needed to train successfully. It becomes a guiding force that helps you transform setbacks into steps forward and fuels your determination to succeed through calm observation of what is really going on.

Mindfulness is known to reduce stress, and a less stressed trainer makes for a less stressed dog. Dog training can be physically and emotionally demanding, and it's important to take breaks and practice self-care activities, such as exercise or relaxation techniques, to reduce stress and improve patience. There are courses online for this, and they are also available within our member's area.

I see mindfulness as an essential skill for all trainers to master. It is the foundation for all other skills and techniques used in dog training. Mindfulness allows trainers to connect with their dogs and respond appropriately to their needs, promoting a positive and successful training experience.

Mindfulness and mindset play a key role in dog training. Acknowledging their importance, the Ladies Working Dog Group (LWDG) has woven them into the core of its membership framework.

I believe that training isn't just about giving commands and expecting obedience. Instead, it's about understanding and connection. When trainers are mindful, they are more in tune with their own emotions and reactions, as well as with the dog's needs and responses. This makes training more effective and reduces misunderstandings.

For example, if a dog doesn't follow a command, instead of getting angry, a mindful trainer would try to understand why. Maybe the dog is distracted, unsure, or just not ready for what you are asking. By being aware of these nuances, you can adjust your approach. By promoting this mindset, LWDG ensures its members are not just skilled in training techniques, but also experienced at building strong, understanding relationships with their dogs.

WHY YOU SHOULDN'T PARK WHEN YOU'RE ON THE MOTORWAY

Imagine life as a motorway journey. You're on the open road, cruising along at a good speed, with the wind in your hair and your favourite music playing. Everything's moving smoothly, just as planned.

Then suddenly, out of nowhere, you hit a speed bump — let's call this a life setback. It shakes you up a bit. But instead of letting it derail you, you pull into a service station, taking a short break to process, recover and plan your next move.

Perhaps you've experienced a personal loss or a professional disappointment. Whatever it is, it's natural, and even necessary, to stop and reflect; to tend to your needs and gather your strength. Then, after this pause, you merge back onto the motorway and continue onwards, enhanced by the lessons from that bump in the road.

But what happens if, after another speed bump, you find yourself stuck in that service station, unable to return to the motorway? This metaphorical service station could be a place of self-doubt, procrastination, fear of failure or even comfort in the familiar. It's easy to become paralysed in these moments, letting setbacks keep us from moving forward.

This metaphor doesn't just apply to life but extends beautifully to your dog training. Your training roadmap is filled with both successes and setbacks. Maybe your dog's recall was flawless one day, only to fail spectacularly the next. Or perhaps, despite all your patience and hard work, your dog just can't seem to master that tricky water retrieve.

When faced with such setbacks, it's tempting to pull into the service station and dwell on what went wrong, or even give up altogether. But here's the thing, just as with life, it's essential not to let these trials make us permanently park up.

It's okay, even necessary, to take a break, regroup and reassess. Perhaps you need to switch up your training techniques, consult with a fellow dog owner or even just give yourself and your dog a day off, but the key is to not let these setbacks deter you from getting back on that motorway and continuing.

Remember, facing difficulty is part of the process of becoming a more skilled and effective owner and trainer. The motorway awaits. Don't let setbacks turn your service station break into a permanent parking spot.

AVOIDING COMPARISON

"Comparisonitus" is a term I use to describe the tendency to compare my dog's training evolution to that of others.

Comparing your dog to others can be a dangerous trap to fall into. Each dog is unique, with their own strengths and weaknesses, and comparing them to others can lead to feelings of inadequacy and unrealistic expectations. Additionally, comparing your dog to others can undermine the progress you and your dog have made.

I've watched dogs from the same litter all train together and their levels of ability, focus and maturity have all been hugely different. Comparing any of them would not be a fair reflection of their future abilities or their possibility to progress as they mature.

Comparing your dog to others can also create an unhelpful competitive mindset, which can damage relationships between handlers and their dogs. Dogs rely on their handlers for guidance and support, and a competitive approach can undermine the bond between them. It's important to focus on your dog's individual progress and celebrate their achievements, rather than comparing them to others.

Comparing our dog's progress to that of others can also have a negative impact on us as trainers. It's easy to fall into the trap of comparing our own ability to that of others, leading to feelings of inadequacy and self-doubt. This can create a vicious cycle of negative self-talk and over-criticism, ultimately hindering our training progress and the bond we have with our dogs. Instead of comparing ourselves to others, it's important to focus on our own progress and learning.

One famous quote I love is by Theodore Roosevelt: ***"Comparison is the thief of joy".*** When we compare ourselves to others, we often focus on what we lack or what we're not good at, and when training, this can be soul-destroying. Instead, I encourage you to focus on your own achievements and strengths rather than comparing yourself to others.

SOCIAL MEDIA STORIES

Social media has made it easier than ever to compare yourself and your dog to others, that said, it's important to remember that social media only presents a curated highlight reel of someone's life at a set moment, and it's not a realistic representation of them, their ability, or their dog training. It's essential to approach social media with a critical eye, recognising that what you see online is not always reflective of reality.

In our modern, interconnected world, social media platforms have become a prominent part of our daily lives. These platforms, while offering numerous benefits, have also made it incredibly easy to compare ourselves, our achievements, and our dogs, with others, yet, it's vital to acknowledge the deceptive nature of social media and how it can distort our perceptions.

When scrolling through a dog training page on social media, you might come across perfectly executed commands, impeccably behaved dogs and trainers who seem to effortlessly succeed. Seeing these curated snippets of life can make you feel like you're falling short in your own dog training. It's essential to remember that these are selected snapshots in time, chosen to be shared with the world. They don't include the countless hours of training, the mistakes, the setbacks or the frustration that may have led to that 'perfect' moment.

Take, for instance, a video of a dog flawlessly performing a water retrieve. The short clip doesn't show the weeks or even months of practice that went into learning that command. It doesn't show the times when the dog was distracted or unresponsive or scared of entering the water. It doesn't show the moments of doubt and frustration the owner might have felt along the way. All it shows is the end result, creating an illusion of perfection that can feel unattainable. It's important to not let these comparisons undermine your progress or discourage you from continuing your training.

Appreciate online content for what it is – a moment of success amidst countless unseen moments of effort, persistence and dedication. Instead of comparing your skill level to those you see online, focus on sharing your own progress and the unique relationship you have with your dog. Celebrate online your achievements, no matter how small they may seem in comparison, and remember that every dog and every trainer have their own pace and their own story. Your experiences with your dog are unique and that's something to be proud of.

UNVEILING REALITY

My writing for Gundog Journal Magazine over the last few years has allowed me to bring to light an essential perspective often overlooked in traditional press and on social media – the hardship of dog training. I write a regular feature entitled "Most Difficult

Moment", which is dedicated to sharing the tough times trainers and their dogs go through. It's not an article of the perfect memories; instead, it's an authentic reflection of the real struggles involved in dog training.

Each story captures someone's hardest training challenge, often marked by disappointment, frustration and even failure. By openly discussing these moments, the feature breaks down the illusion created by social media and in our minds, that training a dog is always smooth sailing. It reveals the perseverance it takes to overcome hurdles and the determination required to keep going even when progress seems elusive.

Reading these articles can provide a dose of reality that can be both refreshing and reassuring. It's a reminder that even the most skilled and experienced of trainers face difficulties and that setbacks are an integral part of the training course. It humanises the often-idealised world of dog training, proving that everyone, no matter how experienced, encounters issues.

When you understand this, it becomes easier to look at those seemingly perfect moments on social media. You start to see past the curated stories and appreciate the effort and patience that goes into each success, big or small. The stories help to create a more accurate and relatable picture of the dog training experience.

The approach I take in my "Most Difficult Moment" column in the Gundog Journal is mirrored within the membership of the LWDG. Our goal is to cultivate an environment that promotes transparency, empathy and a realistic understanding of dog training.

In our community, we encourage members to share not only their successes but also their struggles. We believe that sharing these experiences provides a more realistic picture of what it's like to train a working dog. Just like in the magazine, these shared stories are about real people, with real dogs, facing real challenges. It's about showing that we all have tough days and that it's okay to stumble and fall.

The shared experiences within the LWDG not only bring about a sense of camaraderie among members but also create an environment of learning and growth. When one member shares a barrier they're facing, others will offer advice, suggest solutions or simply provide words of encouragement. This way, our members can learn from each other's experiences, which can be incredibly valuable.

Moreover, these shared experiences often lead to breakthroughs in training. They allow members to gain new perspectives and ideas, inspiring them to try different approaches with their dogs. It's also not unusual for members to find comfort and relief in knowing they're not alone in their struggles.

Knowing that others have faced similar difficulties can also provide a sense of solidarity and community. It reminds you that it's okay to have hard days. It can foster a more compassionate and patient approach towards yourself and your dog, reducing the tendency to over-criticise and fostering a more constructive, understanding mindset.

Understanding the true and honest stories of many dog trainers can encourage you to navigate your own way with more confidence. It allows you to appreciate your unique pathway with your dog, celebrate your progress and approach dilemmas with an ever-evolving perspective. And that is a story worth sharing.

CREATING AND USING AFFIRMATIONS FOR SUCCESS

Affirmations are simple, positive statements that are intended to encourage and motivate us to achieve our intentions. They can be incredibly helpful for building confidence, self-belief and a more positive mindset. When used consistently and genuinely, affirmations can lead to tremendous growth and success and can silence critical self-talk in seconds. Where the mantra "If I am the problem, I am also the solution" focuses on halting our negative thoughts and reframing them, affirmations are very much about introducing far more positive thinking into our lives.

I must admit, there was a time when I found the concept of affirmations rather silly. I couldn't wrap my head around the idea that repeating positive statements over and over for endless days could have any real impact on my life. Still, I'm open-minded and gave it a try and, as time went on and I gained more experience and knowledge, I began to see the value in affirmations. I began to think more positively across all areas of my life without needing to be consciously aware of it.

Observing successful people who incorporated affirmations into their daily routines showed me that these simple, yet powerful statements could indeed make a difference. As I embraced affirmations myself, I discovered their transformative potential in cultivating my confidence, self-belief, and a more positive mindset.

Incorporating powerful and positive statements into your daily routine can have profound effects on your mindset and overall well-being. These affirmations serve as tools to redirect your thoughts, help you overcome self-doubt and build confidence in your abilities not only as a dog owner but in all aspects of life.

It all begins with acknowledging the power of your thoughts, as we have discussed throughout this book. Your thoughts shape your feelings, your actions and consequently, your results.

If you're constantly drowning in negative thoughts about yourself or your dog's capabilities, it can become a self-fulfilling prophecy. On the other hand, by consciously directing your thoughts towards positivity and self-belief, you can cultivate an internal environment that nurtures growth and success.

When creating your affirmations, start by focusing on your intentions. Reflect on your aspirations as a working dog owner, considering the skills you want to improve, the relationship you want to build with your dog, and the milestones you hope to achieve. Be specific and positive when crafting your affirmations, using language that clearly outlines your desired outcomes. To illustrate, instead of saying, "I won't be nervous at competitions," say, "I am confident and calm at competitions".

It's important to frame your affirmations in the present tense, as if you've already achieved your goals. This approach helps your mind accept the statements as true, fostering a sense of renewed motivation. Make your affirmations personal by including your dog's name or other details that make the statements uniquely yours.

Here are a few examples of affirmations for working dog owners to get you started:

"My dog, Fido, and I make an excellent team."
"I am patient and understanding with my Fido."
"I am capable and confident in my ability to train Fido."
"Fido responds well to my instructions."
"Every day, Fido and I are learning and growing together."
"I trust Fido, and Fido trusts me."
"I handle challenges with Fido calmly and effectively."
"I am a responsible and caring dog owner."
"My bond with Fido grows stronger every day."
"I celebrate the progress Fido and I make, no matter how small."
"I am grateful for the positive impact Fido has on my life."
"Fido and I understand each other."
"Training Fido is a rewarding experience."
"Fido and I enjoy our training sessions."
"I am proud of the progress Fido and I have made."
"I am always open to learning new ways to train and care for Fido."
"Fido's trust in me strengthens our bond."

"I respond to issues with Fido in a positive and constructive way."
"I appreciate the unique qualities of Fido."
"Together, Fido and I can overcome any training tests and trials."

To effectively use affirmations for success, consistency is key. Set aside time each day to recite your affirmations, whether it's during your morning routine, on your way to training, or before bed. As you repeat your affirmations, visualise yourself and your dog achieving your goals. This mental imagery strengthens the connection between your affirmations and your desired outcomes. Embrace the emotions that accompany your affirmations, as this emotional connection can make your affirmations more powerful and effective.

Finally, keep your affirmations visible by writing them on sticky notes, recording them as a voice note, or creating a digital reminder, and place them where you'll see them regularly. This constant reinforcement can help you maintain a positive mindset throughout the day, encouraging you and your dog to reach new heights in your training. Remember, the journey of working with your dog is a unique and personal experience. Embrace the power of affirmations. In doing so, you'll not only enhance your bond with your dog but also create an environment where both of you can thrive.

CHAPTER SNAPSHOT:

- Recognise the dangers of over-criticising your dog and yourself and the negative impact it can have on your training progress.
- Set realistic expectations for your dog, based on their breed, age and personality, and focus on progress and intentions rather than specific goals.
- Be patient with yourself and your dog, understanding that learning new skills takes time and practice.
- Avoid 'comparisonitus' by focusing on your own dog's progress and learning pathway.
- Celebrate your dog's unique personality and individual progress, avoiding labels such as "stubborn" or "uncooperative."
- Stay positive and encouraging during training sessions, even if your dog isn't getting it right away.
- Enjoy training your dog. Each time, it strengthens the bond between you.

READER EXERCISES

1. Identify a negative thought or belief that you have about yourself as a dog owner and dispute it with evidence to the contrary.
2. Create a list of affirmations that resonate with you and use them daily to counter negative self-talk.

FINAL THOUGHTS...

As someone who has experienced the negative impact of over-criticism first-hand, I understand the importance of developing patience and a positive mindset in dog training. Through my work with the Ladies Working Dog Group, I have seen the incredible power of celebrating progress and setting realistic intentions, rather than getting caught up in the pressures of comparison and perfectionism.

By staying mindful and focusing on the unique needs of each individual dog, we can create a more compassionate and effective training environment, one that consistently strengthens the bond between handler and canine companion and unlocks the full potential of both.

With dedication, patience and kindness, you can create a fulfilling partnership that will give you hours and hours of joy, sprinkled with fewer and fewer moments of frustration as you grow better together.

CHAPTER 7
FINDING THE SILVER LININGS

The idea for the Ladies Working Dog Group was born during a particularly challenging time in my life when I was grappling with the effects of PTSD and struggling to find my own confidence and self-belief. At that low point, I was encouraged to embark on a journey with my own working dog. My family hoped it would help me to find some solace and purpose in the process.

As I delved into the world of shooting and began training and working alongside my dog, a remarkable transformation took place. I discovered an unforeseen sense of purpose and a renewed passion for life. Working with my dog not only helped me cope with my struggles but also equipped me to face life's other obstacles with a newfound optimism. This optimism became the silver lining in my life, giving me hope.

That's why I believe that finding the silver lining is such an important mindset for owners. When we approach training, and life in general, with a positive attitude, we're better equipped to overcome the significant setbacks we are bound to face.

Let me share a personal anecdote to illustrate this point. My dog, Ella, used to struggle to retrieve a dummy, as she simply had no interest. After two or three retrieves, she would literally just stop. No matter what I tried, Ella didn't seem interested. Retrieving dummies simply didn't excite her. No amount of coaxing or changing techniques seemed to make a difference. But, observing her love for tennis balls, an idea took root. This spark of inspiration led to the creation of the **LWDG Tennis Ball Wrap.**

To bring this idea to life, we collaborated with Sporting Saint, a leading specialist from the UK, known for their wonderful gundog training equipment. Originating from the dedicated efforts of Philippa Jones, Sporting Saint emerged from a kitchen table in Herefordshire in 2007. Pip's profound passion for gundogs and producing the high-quality equipment needed to train them, made her company a perfect fit for our innovative idea. By incorporating our new Tennis Ball Wrap, made by Sporting Saint, into her training sessions, I was able to build Ella's excitement and eventually transition her love of tennis balls over into training with dummies.

We didn't just solve Ella's problem; we found a solution for many others too. By covering the middle of any dummy with this fab tennis felt wrap, pups and dogs with a drive for tennis balls can easily transfer over to anything you can wrap. A silver lining for sure. This shows that dog training challenges can often lead to new and creative fixes.

By finding every silver lining and incorporating ideas into our dog training, we can turn setbacks into opportunities, strengthen our relationships with our working dogs and discover new ways to overcome obstacles. In the end, it's all about maintaining a positive outlook, even when things get tough.

YOUR PAST CANNOT TELL YOUR FUTURE

In the journey of life and in the world of working dog training, the past plays a significant role. It serves as a valuable teacher, imparting valuable lessons and wisdom from the experiences we've encountered. However, it is essential to understand that the past is merely a teacher, not a fortune teller.

Reflecting on your past experiences can be a powerful tool for improvement. We can learn from our successes and mistakes, understanding what approaches worked well and what didn't. The past can offer insights into the training methods that brought about the best results. It helps you recognise patterns and tendencies in both your dogs' behaviour and your responses, allowing you to make more informed decisions in the present. It helps you to find the silver linings in what you have done so far.

While the past is a valuable teacher, it is necessary to remember that it cannot predict the future. Each dog we work with is a new and distinct entity, and their journey is inherently different from any dog we've encountered before. Attempting to use the past as a fortune teller, by assuming that similar situations will always yield the same outcomes, can limit our ability to embrace new possibilities whilst hindering our growth.

When you rely too heavily on the past as a future predictor, you become hesitant to take risks or try new approaches in training. Fear of repeating past mistakes can hold you back from exploring methods that could be better suited to your current dog's needs. It is essential to strike a balance between drawing on the lessons of the past and embracing the potential for growth and change in the present and future. Honouring the past as a teacher while being aware of its limitations as the 'only' way to train is essential for personal and professional development.

By drawing on the wisdom of your experiences, and that of others with their dogs, you can improve your training methods. At the same time, remaining open to new possibilities allows us to embrace the potential for transformation that lies ahead. Let the past be your teacher and guide, but never let it dictate your future.

PERSEVERANCE PAYS OFF

By now you should be completely aware of the moments of frustration, disappointment and self-doubt you will (or are) going to face. Maintaining an unwavering commitment to your dog's training and your development will ultimately lead to the reward of a well-behaved, reliable partner.

Perseverance and resilience are not the same thing.

Perseverance refers to the ability to keep doing something despite challenges. It's about persistence, determination and the willingness to keep trying and not give up even when things get tough. If you're training a dog and they are struggling with a new command, it's your perseverance that keeps you working at it, adjusting your methods and not giving up until your dog masters it.

On the other hand, resilience refers to the ability to bounce back from adversity or tricky situations. It's about mental toughness and adaptability. If you face a setback in your training with your dog - let's say your dog falls ill, or an unexpected event disrupts your regular training routine - your resilience is what allows you to adapt, recover, and return to training once the situation improves.

Both perseverance and resilience are critical in dog training, and in life in general. Perseverance allows you to keep moving forward and make progress, while resilience enables you to handle setbacks and changes in a constructive and healthy way. Both qualities can be developed and strengthened with conscious effort and practice.

PLAN, DO, REVIEW

Planning and reviewing are essential components of persevering in your training. By setting aside time to plan your training sessions, you can ensure that you have clear objectives and a structured approach. This can help you stay focused and motivated as you work towards your goals.

Many years ago, at the start of my new training journey with my dogs, I often found myself tangled in a web of tasks, reminders and reflections. Remembering what training I had done, deciphering what still needed addressing and carving out moments for self-reflection became paramount. While a basic notebook could serve as a repository for these scattered thoughts, I felt the need for a more structured tool — one that would not just document, but also guide and inspire me.

Thus, the LWDG Magic Month Planner was born, a product of personal necessity and passion. More than just a planner, it's a comprehensive system I designed to help fellow trainers and dog owners alike. It aids in organising, planning and tracking your dog goals, daily tasks and habits. More importantly, it provides ample space for reflection, acting as a tool to foster mindfulness, track progress and boost self-confidence.

While any tool or notebook can document, the LWDG Magic Month Planner is about creating a dedicated space for your journey with your dog, ensuring that every step taken is purposeful, every lesson learned is noted and every achievement is celebrated.

Whether using a simple notebook or a dedicated planner, planning and reflective work can help individuals stay focused, motivated, and on track towards achieving their desired outcomes.

Additionally, regularly reviewing your progress allows you to identify areas where you may need to adjust your approach or dedicate more time to training. This reflection can help you remain committed to your goals, even when the going gets tough.

WHAT IS MY INTENTION?

Creating an intention list is another way to reinforce your commitment to your dog's training. This list should include specific actions and attitudes you intend to adopt during your training sessions. For example, you might include "be patient and kind" or "focus on positive reinforcement". Referring to your intention list before each session can help you maintain a positive mindset and stay on track, even when you face difficulty. By reminding yourself of your intentions, you can maintain a positive mindset and avoid getting frustrated or discouraged.

Rewarding yourself for hitting milestones in your training is another great way to keep going. These rewards can be the silver lining to the work done. Recognising your achievements and celebrating them, whether it's by something simple like treating yourself to a favourite snack or indulging in some well-deserved new dog equipment, can help you stay motivated and committed to your dog's training. This positive reinforcement for your own efforts will encourage you to continue working towards your intentions/goals, no matter how challenging they may seem.

Finding and fostering friendships within the working dog community can be a tremendous source of support and encouragement. These friendships are some of the best silver linings of our sport. Connecting with like-minded individuals who share your passion for working dogs can provide you with invaluable advice, inspiration and camaraderie. These friendships can help you stay accountable, offer a sounding board for your struggles and successes, and provide a sense of belonging that can help you persevere through difficult times.

By incorporating new ideas such as planning and reviewing, creating an intention list, rewarding yourself for hitting milestones and finding and fostering friendships, you'll be in a stronger position to navigate the forthcoming highs and lows. In the end, it's the unwavering dedication and commitment to your dog's development that will pave the way for a lifelong partnership.

NAVIGATING THE SILVER LININGS IN EVERY SITUATION

As the famous quote by Elizabeth Edwards goes,

> *"She stood in the storm, and when the wind did not blow her way, she adjusted her sails."*

Finding the 'silver linings' in every situation might seem like a daunting task, especially when faced with a consistently difficult dog. However, it's a habit that can be nurtured over time, and the benefits it brings to your relationship with your dog and to your own personal development are immense.

Start by shifting your perspective. Instead of viewing a situation as solely negative, consider what can be learned from it. Each obstacle presents an opportunity to gain new insights, whether it's about your dog's behaviour, your own response to stress, or even a new approach to training that you hadn't considered before.

For instance, if your dog is struggling with a particular command, instead of seeing this as a failure, look at it as a chance to understand your dog's learning style better. Your dog may respond better to visual cues rather than verbal ones, or they may need more repetition to understand a command. By changing your perspective, you turn a seemingly negative situation into a chance for learning and growth.

Practice mindfulness as discussed earlier. Paying closer attention to the present moment can help you notice subtleties that you might otherwise overlook. By being fully present during your time with your dog, you can better observe their reactions, pick up on their cues and ultimately gain a deeper understanding of them. This newfound awareness can reveal the silver linings that were hidden in plain sight all along.

Remember to show yourself compassion. Finding silver linings isn't about glossing over difficulties or ignoring your feelings. It's perfectly normal to feel frustrated or upset when facing a setback. However, by treating yourself with kindness and understanding, you create a safe space to explore these feelings, understand them, and ultimately transform them into an ever-expanding growth mindset.

Finally, practice gratitude. Gratitude helps us focus on the positive aspects of our lives and it's a powerful tool for finding silver linings. Take a moment each day to reflect on the things you appreciate about your dog and the joy they bring to your life. This habit can help you keep your problems in perspective.

In the grand scheme of things, finding the silver linings in every training session is about more than just remaining optimistic. It's a mindset that nurtures your resilience, promotes a deeper connection with your dog and transforms trials into opportunities.

OVERCOMING FEAR AND SELF-DOUBT

Fear and self-doubt are other common emotions that many working dog owners experience during training. Overcoming these feelings and building confidence in both you and your dog are essential for developing a strong and trusting partnership. By overcoming these fears, you can more easily find the good in everything.

Fear is a powerful and primal emotion. It can be a beneficial tool when we face real, immediate danger, triggering our 'fight or flight' response, but it can be detrimental too. It's had me so afraid,

I wouldn't leave the house for days on end. This is why Dad first took me out with the dogs, to try to break the habit of staying in, where I felt safe. My fear had become overwhelming and paralysing, causing me to retreat into my comfort zone and avoid situations that made me anxious or scared.

I had truly little interest in the world beyond my doorstep. I found solace in the familiarity of my home, where I felt protected from the unknown 'dangers' that lurked outside. It was a vicious cycle, as the more I avoided facing my fears, the stronger they seemed to become.

Worried about the impact this fear was having on my life, my dad introduced me to a new experience: Beating. Beating with a dog refers to a specific role within field sports, particularly in driven game shooting. The primary function of the beaters and their dogs is to move through terrain, like woodlands or fields, to flush out game. A well-trained dog in this role is invaluable, as it can effectively locate and move game from areas that might be challenging for humans alone. The bond and coordination between the beater and their dog are essential for a successful day.

Dad knew that the dogs would provide a comforting presence, acting as a source of companionship and support as I ventured outside. This simple act was a profound step towards breaking free from the clutches of my anxiety.

Never one for doing things slowly, Dad threw me in at the deep end. The first day out shooting was chaotic but watching the dogs work kept me from worrying. The dogs acted as a bridge between me and the outside world, drawing my attention away from my fear and redirecting it towards their needs and the joy of their company. I was hooked.

Through the following days out with Dad, I learned that fear is not an all-encompassing force that should dictate the boundaries of my life. It is something to be acknowledged and respected, but not to be controlled by. Dad's decision to take me out with the dogs was a pivotal moment in my quest towards overcoming my fears. It taught me the importance of facing my anxieties head-on, step by step, and gradually expanding my comfort zone.

Reflecting on those days of retreat within my home, I'm thankful not for the fear itself, but for the strength I discovered in overcoming it. It's shown me the depths of my own resilience and the potential for growth that can only be accessed beyond the walls of fear. Today, I continue to explore the world with a sense of bravery and curiosity, knowing that every step I take is a triumph over the fear that once held me captive.

When fear lingers or grows out of proportion, it can cloud your vision and hinder your ability to see the potential positive aspects or "silver linings" in challenging situations.

The reason fear can be such a potent silver-lining destroyer is twofold. First, fear tends to narrow our focus. When we're afraid, we're more likely to fixate on potential threats or negative outcomes, often exaggerating them. This can make it harder for us to see beyond the immediate problem and recognise the opportunities for growth or learning that may also be present. There was no imminent danger outside my home, but I convinced myself it was there. And we do this when we train too. We scare ourselves that it's all going to go catastrophically wrong.

For example, if you're worried about your dog's performance in a forthcoming working test, your fear might lead you to overlook the progress your dog has made and the skills you've both gained in preparation for the event. You let yourself fail mentally before you start physically.

Fear often fuels negativity and encourages a 'worst-case scenario' mindset. This can lead us to expect failure or disappointment, which, in turn, can dampen our motivation and drive. If we believe that our dog training efforts will inevitably lead to failure because of past setbacks, we might give up before we've given ourselves a fair chance to succeed.

Overcoming fear is key to uncovering the bright side of every circumstance. This doesn't mean we should ignore or suppress our fears; instead, it involves acknowledging them, understanding where they come from, and then using tools such as mindfulness, positive affirmations and patience to challenge and manage them.

PRACTISING SELF-COMPASSION

Practising self-compassion is another vital aspect of your progression. By treating yourself with kindness, understanding and empathy, you create a supportive internal environment that helps you navigate setbacks and discover hidden opportunities for growth and connection.

One of the key reasons why self-compassion is important is that it allows you to view difficulties through a lens of understanding and kindness. Rather than dwelling on perceived failures or shortcomings, self-compassion encourages you to acknowledge your efforts and progress. It shifts your focus from self-criticism to self-acceptance, enabling you to learn from the obstacles you encounter. Through self-compassion, setbacks become valuable learning experiences rather than sources of discouragement.

Practising self-compassion is also rooted in the recognition of your own humanity and imperfections. It involves embracing the fact that you are not meant to be perfect. Mistakes and setbacks are inevitable, and they are a natural part of the learning routeway. Self-compassion enables you to approach these moments with understanding and forgiveness, rather than self-criticism. It allows you to view yourself with the same empathy and compassion you would offer to a close friend or loved one, fostering a positive and nurturing relationship with yourself.

Opening up about my fears, thoughts and personal experiences has always been hard for me. For a long time, I hesitated, fearing judgment or misunderstanding. It felt as though, by exposing my innermost feelings, I was revealing a part of myself that was fragile and could easily be hurt. The walls I built around these emotions were a protective tool, ensuring that I remained shielded from criticism or pain.

However, as time went on, I began to realise the immense power of sharing. Each time I dared to be vulnerable, not only did I pave a path for my own healing, but I also, inadvertently, became a beacon for others. By sharing my story, I gave others the courage to share theirs. It was a domino effect of shared experiences, mutual understanding and profound connection.

I've come to learn that in being vulnerable, in letting down those walls, I not only help myself, but I provide comfort to others. They see that they aren't alone in their struggles or feelings. It's a shared relationship of growth, where my openness becomes a catalyst for others to reflect, connect and heal. Sharing, despite its initial challenges, has become a transformative tool in my journey, reshaping how I connect with myself and those around me.

LWDG Mindset Coach Emma Liddell plays a huge role in my ongoing work toward self-compassion. When I expressed my frustrations about a tough training session recently, her response, "Why are you talking about my friend like that?", hit me hard.

Emma's simple question was a wake-up call. It showed me that I had been too hard on myself. Her kind words encouraged me to be nicer to myself, just like I would be to a good friend. I started to speak to myself more gently, both in life and during my gundog training. Thanks to Emma, I now understand how vital it is to be kind to myself while talking about my journey.

Another important aspect of self-compassion is setting realistic expectations. Take time to acknowledge your own limits and, as we've already discussed, avoid comparing your progress to others. Self-compassion encourages you to set achievable intentions/goals and celebrate small victories along the way. By acknowledging and appreciating your own progress, you create an environment of self-support and encouragement.

Finally, self-compassion extends beyond training sessions and incorporates self-care. Taking care of yourself physically, emotionally and mentally is a fundamental aspect of self-compassion. It involves engaging in activities that rejuvenate you and provide a sense of fulfilment outside of dog training. By prioritising self-care, you affirm your own worth and acknowledge that your well-being is just as important as your dog's training progress.

Come on, admit it, we all know the truth. Sometimes, we treat our dogs better than we treat ourselves. Just think about it. When did you last buy your dog a gift? Perhaps it was that gorgeous drying coat or that dummy to go with the other forty you cart about in your bag.

Now, contrast that with the last time you bought yourself something purely out of self-love. No, that emergency coffee to survive Monday morning doesn't count! Nor does that piece of toast for dinner as you forgot to go shopping (again) because you were in the middle of a woodland somewhere when you should have been in the supermarket. When did you pamper yourself like you do your beloved dog?

It's almost as if our dogs are living the VIP life, getting the red carpet treatment everywhere they go, while we've stuck ourselves on the sidelines, cheering them on, forgetting to treat ourselves with the same enthusiasm. Next time, while buying that fancy leather dog collar, you should grab a matching belt for yourself because hey, if your dog is the king or queen, shouldn't you at least be the royal advisor with some bling? I will confess, as I write these words of wisdom, my dogs lay around the house in better beds than the humans do, so maybe I need to take my own advice more!

FINDING THE BRIGHT SIDE

Understanding the distinction between probability and possibility can benefit your training of your dog. While both concepts involve uncertain outcomes, they have different implications that can shape your approach to training and decision-making.

Probability refers to the likelihood of a specific outcome occurring based on past experiences or statistical data. It involves assessing the chances of a particular event happening and making informed predictions. In dog training, probability can come into play when determining the success of certain commands or behaviours based on previous training sessions. By analysing the probability of your dog responding correctly, you can adjust your training techniques or strategies.

On the other hand, possibility encompasses a broader range of potential outcomes, including those that may be less likely but still plausible. It involves being open to different scenarios and embracing the idea that unexpected situations can arise. In dog training, acknowledging possibility can help you anticipate and adapt to unpredictable circumstances, such as encountering new environments, distractions or obstacles. By embracing possibility, you can be prepared for various scenarios and better equipped to handle them effectively.

Understanding the difference between what's likely and what's possible in dog training helps you stay grounded yet open to new methods. By looking at past behaviours, you can predict what might happen next, but by also staying open to new possibilities, you ensure your training remains flexible and adaptable.

For instance, if your dog consistently retrieves objects during training sessions, the probability of a successful retrieve may be high. However, acknowledging the possibility of encountering unfamiliar environments or unusual behaviours can help you prepare your dog for potential problems. By using different training settings, introducing unexpected distractions and simulating realistic scenarios, you can enhance your dog's abilities and ensure they are prepared for a wide range of possibilities in the field.

Understanding the difference between probability and possibility in gundog training can be so valuable. By balancing these concepts, you can develop a well-rounded training approach that prepares you and your dog for both likely and unexpected situations. This awareness helps you to not be caught out so easily and trains you to expect the unexpected and to use this awareness to have more fun than fear in sessions.

THE POWER OF COMMUNITY

One of the most effective ways to uncover silver linings in your training is to immerse yourself in a community of like-minded individuals who share your passion and commitment. A supportive network of fellow dog owners can provide invaluable encouragement, advice and inspiration, making the roadblocks you face less daunting and the entire experience more enjoyable.

The LWDG facilitates an environment where women can lean on each other for support, transforming their training outcomes. Being part of a community like the LWDG allows you to connect with others who have faced similar difficulties and triumphs in their training sessions. This shared understanding creates a sense of camaraderie and empathy, ensuring that you never feel alone in your struggles or achievements. By exchanging stories and experiences with fellow dog owners, you can learn from their successes and setbacks, discovering new silver linings and opportunities for growth.

A supportive community offers a wealth of knowledge and expertise, providing valuable insights and guidance to help you navigate the complexities of working dog training. The LWDG, for example, connects its members with experienced trainers, informative resources and a platform for asking questions and seeking advice. By tapping into this collective wisdom, you can enhance your own training techniques, overcome obstacles and uncover positive aspects in the form of newfound knowledge and strategies.

Training a working dog can be an emotional rollercoaster, with moments of joy and pride often accompanied by frustration and self-doubt. A supportive community can be a lifeline during these challenging times, offering encouragement and reassurance to help you maintain a positive mindset. Knowing that you have a network of fellow dog owners cheering you on can be a powerful motivator, inspiring you to persevere through difficult moments and uncover the unseen benefits that lie beneath.

In addition to providing support during challenging times, a strong community also serves as a space for celebrating your accomplishments and milestones. Sharing your successes with fellow dog owners can not only boost your own confidence but also inspire others to push through their struggles and strive for their goals. This collective sense of accomplishment can foster a positive and uplifting atmosphere, helping you to see the silver linings in even the most challenging situations.

The power of community cannot be underestimated when it comes to finding silver linings. By surrounding yourself with a supportive network of fellow dog owners, you'll gain access to shared experiences, valuable advice, emotional encouragement and a space for celebrating achievements. Through the Ladies Working Dog Group and similar communities, you can transform your training into a more enjoyable and rewarding experience, filled with unexpected moments of delight and lifelong friendships.

THE TRUE MEANING OF SILVER LININGS IN DOG TRAINING

Discovering the silver linings in your training involves a combination of mindset, community support and an appreciation for both the small victories and the bigger picture. Through practising self-compassion, turning to fellow dog owners for inspiration and support, celebrating your progress and focusing on the lifelong impact of your training efforts, you'll become more competent at uncovering the hidden opportunities and rewards within every adversity.

In the process of training your dog, it's essential to take the time to celebrate small victories and acknowledge the progress you and your dog are making. These small milestones, whether it's a successful recall or a smooth retrieve, serve as markers of growth and development, providing motivation and encouragement as you continue. By focusing on and celebrating these small wins, you'll not only build your confidence, but also strengthen the bond between you and your dog.

To truly appreciate the small victories, keep the wins in your training journal to track your progress and reflect on the improvements you've made. This practice will help you maintain a positive mindset and remind you of how far you've come, even when you’ve faced huge training hurdles. Celebrating these achievements, no matter how small, can reveal the silver linings and inspire you to keep pushing forward.

CHAPTER SNAPSHOT:

- Embrace a positive mindset: Approach your working dog training journey with a focus on growth, learning and resilience. Look for silver linings and use setbacks as opportunities for improvement.
- Practise self-compassion: Treat yourself with kindness, understanding and empathy throughout your training journey. Acknowledge that setbacks are natural and use them to deepen your connection with your dog and refine your training techniques.
- Celebrate small victories: Take the time to acknowledge and celebrate your progress and achievements, no matter how small. This will help boost your confidence and motivation and strengthen the bond between you and your dog.
- Keep a training journal: Track your progress and reflect on your successes by maintaining a journal. This practice will help you stay focused on your goals, appreciate your growth and remind you of how far you've come.
- Connect with a supportive community: Join a network of fellow dog owners, such as the Ladies Working Dog Group, to share experiences, seek advice and find encouragement.
- Focus on the bigger picture: Remember the lifelong impact of a well-trained working dog and the strong, fulfilling partnership that you're building.
- Reflect on your journey regularly: Take the time to reflect on your experiences, obstacles and successes. Use these reflections to uncover silver linings, learn from your experiences and plan for future growth and development in your training journey.

READER EXERCISES

1. Write about a challenge you've faced in your dog ownership journey and identify any positive outcomes or growth that resulted from it.
2. Create a list of "lessons learned" from past failures or setbacks and use them as reminders for future hurdles.

FINAL THOUGHTS...

As we reach the end of this chapter together, I hope you've gained a deeper understanding of the importance of finding silver linings in your training. They're not just a source of encouragement; they're pivotal in shaping a rewarding and enduring relationship with your dog. As you continue with your working dog, I encourage you to maintain a positive and resilient mindset, cherish your achievements and lean on your fellow dog owners for encouragement and inspiration. Remember that the development of your dog may be filled with ups and downs, but it's these shared experiences that ultimately make every moment worth it.

CHAPTER 8
MANAGING WHAT YOU CAN'T CONTROL

Life enjoys throwing curveballs at us, especially when we're working with our four-legged partners. We already know we can't control every aspect of our dog's lives or the world around us, so learning to manage what you can't control is a vital skill for any working dog owner. It teaches us to adapt to the unexpected, grow in confidence and find creative solutions to the problems we face.

Accepting that some things are beyond our control doesn't mean we're powerless; it's an acknowledgement that we can only do so much and that sometimes, the best way to deal with a situation is to go with the flow. I remember a particularly challenging day when I was out on an estate with my dad. Dad had his most trusted and amazing trialling dogs with him. Suddenly, a flock of black geese appeared right in front of us, and his three best dogs ran in and started pulling at tail feathers! Dad was absolutely mortified. At that moment, I realised that no matter how much I prepared or trained, I couldn't control every aspect of our environment.

This chapter is all about learning to embrace this unpredictability and grow from the experience. By the end, you'll feel more confident and capable of handling whatever life and your working dog throw your way. So, let's dive in and start exploring how to make the most of the unexpected twists and turns.

UNDERSTANDING THE LIMITS OF CONTROL

Recognising there are aspects of our dogs' lives and training that we can control, and others that we can't, allows us to focus our energy on what truly matters and avoid unnecessary frustration.

Common scenarios that you can control include your dog's training, feeding schedules and socialisation. You decide when and how to train your dog, what to feed them and how often they interact with other dogs and people. These aspects of their lives are within your sphere of influence, and you have the power to shape their experiences and development.

On the other hand, there are several factors you can't control. These include the weather, other animals and unexpected distractions (like the geese). For example, you can't predict when a squirrel will dart across your dog's path, or when a sudden downpour might interrupt your training session. It's important to distinguish between what you can and can't control, as this awareness allows you to be more prepared and adaptable when facing the tests of training.

ACCEPTING YOUR DOG'S INDIVIDUALITY

I've already touched upon a dog's unique characteristics, which are shaped by a combination of factors, including breed, genetics and individual experiences. It's essential to accept and embrace your dog's individuality, as this will allow you to tailor your training approach to suit their needs.

Breed and genetics play a significant role in shaping a dog's behaviour. Take, for instance, a Border Collie may be more inclined to herd, while a Labrador Retriever may have a stronger drive to retrieve. These instinctive tendencies are important to consider when developing a training plan, as working with your dog's natural instincts will lead to greater success and a happier partnership.

It's crucial to remember that there is no 'one-size-fits-all' approach to training. Instead, focus on understanding and training the dog in front of you. This may mean adjusting your expectations or trying new techniques, but the result will be a stronger bond and a more fulfilling relationship with your dog.

Embracing your dog's individuality also means recognising their limitations and appreciating their progress. Not every dog will excel at the same tasks or learn at the same pace and that's perfectly okay. Celebrate your dog's successes, no matter how big or small, and remember that you are both on an expedition of growth and discovery.

Understanding the limits of control and accepting your dog's individuality are essential steps in becoming a successful working dog owner. By focusing on what you can control and embracing your dog's unique characteristics, you'll be in a stronger position to navigate the unpredictability world.

STRATEGIES FOR COPING WITH THE UNCONTROLLABLE

One of the most important strategies for coping with the uncontrollable is adopting a flexible mindset. I can't stress enough how important being adaptable and willing to change your approach is to maintaining a positive attitude and making progress with your working dog.

A flexible mindset is about being adaptable and open to change, adjusting to new situations as they arise. On the other hand, a growth mindset believes in the ability to learn and improve over time. While flexibility deals with navigating change, growth centres on personal development and progress. Both mindsets offer unique benefits in facing issues and seizing opportunities.

A flexible mindset can benefit both you and your dog in various situations. To illustrate, if you're training outdoors and the weather suddenly changes, being willing to adjust your training plan on-the-fly can prevent frustration and ensure that you're making the most of your time together. Similarly, if your dog is struggling with a particular command, a flexible mindset will allow you to try different techniques until you find one that works for your unique canine companion.

Some practical tips for being prepared for unexpected situations include carrying a first aid kit with essential items such as bandages, antiseptic wipes and tweezers. This will ensure that you can quickly address any minor injuries that may occur during training or outings. Accidents are, by their nature, unexpected and can cause us the most distress.

Having a backup plan for training sessions is also useful in case your original plan is disrupted. For instance, if you intend to train outdoors but there's a storm, having an indoor training plan can keep you and your dog productive.

Mental preparation is also key in remaining calm and focused. By anticipating potential obstacles and considering how you might adapt to them, you'll be better prepared to handle the situation when it arises. Practising mindfulness techniques, such as deep breathing and visualisation, can also help you stay composed and centred during difficult moments.

ENJOYING THE WINS

As a dog owner and trainer, it's essential to acknowledge and celebrate progress, even if it's slower than expected or not exactly what you had planned. Recognising your dog's achievements, no matter how small, helps build confidence and maintains a positive atmosphere during training.

Over the years, being a part of the LWDG has been a truly enriching experience. Witnessing the small victories of our members has taught me invaluable lessons about perseverance, adaptability and the power of community.

As we share our triumphs and support one another, I am constantly reminded that even the tiniest of seemingly insignificant accomplishments can contribute to our growth and confidence as working dog owners. Together, we celebrate these moments and, in doing so, we inspire and uplift each other to continue striving for success with our beloved canine partners.

By acknowledging these small victories, you not only bolster your dog's self-esteem, but also remind yourself of the progress you've made together. This sense of accomplishment can motivate you to keep pushing forward, even when the going gets tough.

'PAW-SITIVE' REINFORCEMENT: IT'S NOT JUST FOR DOGS

Positive reinforcement isn't just for training your dog; it can also be an effective tool for training yourself. To apply this principle to your own personal growth, start by setting achievable goals for yourself and acknowledging your accomplishments along the way. Reward yourself when you reach these milestones, whether it's mastering a new training technique or successfully navigating a challenging situation with your dog. The rewards could be as simple as enjoying your favourite treat, taking some time for yourself to relax, or indulging in a hobby you love.

By consistently reinforcing your successes, you build self-confidence and establish a positive feedback loop that encourages further growth and progress. Remember, the same principles that work for your dog can also work for you. By focusing on the positive, you'll cultivate an optimistic mindset that fosters resilience and personal development.

Keep a journal of your progress to help you recognise and appreciate the strides you and your dog have made together. By consistently acknowledging your achievements, you create a supportive and encouraging environment that fosters personal growth and confidence in your ability.

DEVELOPING PROBLEM-SOLVING SKILLS

Cultivating your own problem-solving skills is essential for successfully working with your dog. By honing your ability to think critically and adapt to new situations, you become more self-reliant and better equipped to handle the unpredictable aspects of life with a working dog.

To develop your problem-solving abilities, consider engaging in activities that challenge your mind and encourage creative thinking. This could include participating in workshops, reading books on dog training, or seeking advice from experts in the field. By exposing yourself to new ideas and techniques, you enhance your own ability to devise effective solutions for the obstacles you and your dog may encounter.

BUILDING YOUR DOGS CONFIDENCE THROUGH POSITIVE REINFORCEMENT

Positive reinforcement training is a powerful method for building your dog's confidence and resilience. This approach is based on rewarding your dog for desired behaviours, which helps them understand what is expected of them and encourages them to repeat these actions. By using positive reinforcement, you create a supportive and encouraging environment that allows your dog to feel secure and confident in their abilities.

Practical tips for incorporating positive reinforcement in your training sessions include using treats, toys or praise as rewards for desired behaviours. Be consistent and timely with your rewards, ensuring that your dog associates the positive reinforcement with the specific action you want to encourage.

Additionally, break down complex tasks into smaller steps, rewarding your dog for each successful part. This will help them build a strong foundation of understanding and increase their self-assurance as they progress through their training.

TEACHING YOUR DOG TO DEVELOP PROBLEM-SOLVING SKILLS

Teaching your dog to think critically and solve problems on their own is invaluable for fostering resilience when dealing with unexpected changes. Just like you, when your dog can effectively navigate difficulties and adapt to new situations, they will become more self-reliant and better equipped to handle the unpredictable aspects of life.

To develop your dog's problem-solving abilities, try incorporating exercises and games that encourage them to use their brains and instincts. Remember to be patient and consistent in your approach, celebrating each small success along the way.

EMBRACING THE JOURNEY

it's essential to remember that the path of working with your dog is filled with both difficulty and joy. By adopting a flexible mindset, preparing for the unexpected, building a strong support network, celebrating small victories and fostering resilience in your dog, you'll be in a stronger position.

Embrace the unique experience of working with your dog and remember that you are not alone. As you continue to grow and learn alongside your dog, remember that the most significant victories often come from the smallest moments.

By staying committed to your dog's growth, resilience and well-being, you will forge an unbreakable bond and create a partnership that will bring joy and fulfilment to both your lives. So, take a deep breath, cherish the adventure, and always remember to celebrate the small victories along the way.

CHAPTER SNAPSHOT:

- Embrace the unpredictable: Accept that some things are beyond your control and focus on what you can manage.
- Understand the limits of control: Recognise what you can and can't control and accept your dog's individuality.
- Adopt a flexible mindset: Be adaptable and willing to change your approach when faced with obstacles.
- Prepare for the unexpected: Carry essential items, have backup plans and practice mental preparation techniques.
- Build a strong support network: Connect with other working dog owners, trainers and experts for guidance and camaraderie.
- Celebrate small victories: Acknowledge your progress, even if it's slower than expected or not exactly what you had planned.
- Foster resilience in yourself: Build confidence through positive reinforcement and develop your problem-solving skills.
- Apply positive reinforcement to your own growth: Set achievable goals, reward yourself for accomplishments and cultivate a positive mindset.
- Reflect on your experiences: Learn from past problems and apply those lessons to future situations.
- Stay committed to your personal growth: Cherish the adventure with your dog and remember that support is

available through resources like the Ladies Working Dog Group.

READER EXERCISES

1. Practice mindfulness exercises to help you stay present and focused on what you can control in any given situation.
2. Write a letter to a fellow dog owner, offering support and empathy for a situation they can't control. Read this letter each time you are feeling overwhelmed.

FINAL THOUGHTS...

I want to share some last thoughts from my perspective as a fellow working dog owner who has faced numerous setbacks, including the unpredictable nature of life. Throughout my development, I've experienced the ups and downs of this unique path and have learned valuable lessons that can help you navigate the unpredictable world in which we live.

Embracing the unpredictable, staying adaptable and focusing on personal growth have been the keys to my ability to continue to move forward each day, and they can be yours as well. My experience of living with brain tumours has taught me the importance of patience, resilience and adaptability, as well as the need to cherish the special moments and connections we have with both our human and canine friends. These lessons have proven invaluable.

I understand that dealing with the uncontrollable is not always easy and can sometimes feel impossible but an essential part of our growth and success is to accept the changes outside of our control and work with them. By learning to accept and adapt to life's uncertainties, we can become better equipped to handle the issues that come our way, both in dog training and beyond.

Remember that you are not alone in this adventure and that resilience, adaptability and a positive mindset can make all the difference as you work through the unpredictability that comes with being both a human and a dog owner.

CHAPTER 9
LIMITING BELIEF

There was a time when I doubted myself as a working dog owner. I had taken on the challenge of training my first gundog, but as the days turned into weeks and the weeks into months, I found myself struggling to make progress. I questioned my abilities and my knowledge, feeling overwhelmed by the responsibilities and expectations that came with the role. Little did I know that the biggest obstacle I faced wasn't my dog's behaviour, but my own limiting beliefs.

In Ant Middleton's book, *The Wall,* he highlights the importance of believing in oneself, saying, "THE BIGGEST GIFT we can give ourselves is self-belief. It can't come from anyone else." This means that while it's nice to get approval from others, it's our own confidence that truly pushes us forward. He emphasises that we should focus on building this internally, reminding us that real strength comes from within, even in a world that often values external approval.

IDENTIFYING YOUR LIMITING BELIEFS

Before we can overcome our limiting beliefs, we must first recognise them. Limiting beliefs are deeply ingrained thoughts and assumptions that hold us back from reaching our full potential. They are often rooted in past experiences, societal expectations, or messages we've internalised from others. These beliefs can manifest in many ways, such as:

- "I'm not good enough to train a working dog."
- "I don't have the time or resources to be successful."
- "I'll never be as good as other trainers."

Your limiting beliefs are almost always the exact opposite of the affirmations you need to use. To identify your limiting beliefs, start by reflecting on the thoughts and feelings that arise when you think about training your working dog.

Self-reflection is an important process that involves taking a step back to analyse our thoughts, emotions, decisions and behaviours. It's an introspective journey into our individual experiences, motivations and values. It's not playing judge to the thoughts, but rather being the jury and keeping an open mind.

By examining our actions and their outcomes, we can gain a better understanding of ourselves — our strengths, weaknesses, passions, fears and desires. Self-reflection encourages us to question our beliefs and assumptions, paving the way for personal growth and transformation. It aids in self-awareness, which is the foundation pillar for emotional intelligence. Self-reflection requires honesty, courage and an open mind, as it often reveals uncomfortable truths. And many times, they are truths we don't really want to acknowledge. Nonetheless, it is a powerful tool for self-improvement, helping us align our actions with our goals and values.

Pay attention to any negative or self-defeating thoughts that come to mind. Write them down in a journal or on a piece of paper. This self-reflection can be uncomfortable, but it is an essential step towards growth and change.

Next, consider the origins of these beliefs. Can you trace them back to specific experiences or interactions? In particular, did a childhood teacher or coach undermine your confidence, or did a past failure leave you doubting your abilities? Understanding the roots of your limiting beliefs can help you recognise their irrationality and take steps to dispute them. When we question our beliefs, we allow ourselves to see beyond our assumptions and biases. This process can be really uncomfortable as it can destabilise our sense of certainty and our worldview. It takes us outside of our comfort zone. However, it also opens up opportunities for learning, adapting and evolving. It enables us to discard outdated or limiting beliefs and embrace more strengthening and accurate ones. By questioning our beliefs, we cultivate flexibility in our thinking and pave the way for greater understanding, wisdom and personal growth.

Take time to notice the impact of these beliefs on your training and your relationship with your dog. Are they preventing you from trying new techniques or setting ambitious intentions/goals? Are they causing tension and frustration between you and your dog's development? Acknowledging the consequences of your limiting beliefs can help you understand the importance of overcoming them and motivate you to act.

CHALLENGING YOUR LIMITING BELIEFS

Once you've identified and understood your limiting beliefs, the next step is to challenge and replace them. To do this, you must first question the validity of these beliefs. Just because you think something doesn't make it true. Are your beliefs based on facts or are they interpretations of past experiences? Is there any evidence to support them or are they purely speculative? By critically examining your beliefs, you can begin to see them for what they truly are: self-imposed barriers to your success.

Let's consider a situation where for example you've just adopted a German Shorthaired Pointer, a breed known for their high energy and hunting skills. You might be harbouring the belief, "I can't possibly train a dog as lively and skilled as a GSP".

Remember, this thought is a limiting belief, rooted in your self-doubt, and not a concrete reality. To tackle such a belief, start by questioning its accuracy. Instead of accepting it at face value, challenge it by asking yourself, "Is it an absolute truth that I'm incapable of training this breed of dog?" This thought may seem real due to your initial worry, but it does not define your capabilities or predict your success in training this breed.

Next, recall past instances when you have been successful in handling or training dogs. Any past experiences, irrespective of the breed or size of the dog, are evidence of your abilities. Maybe you've trained a pet before or you've helped a friend with their dog. Your past successes show that you can indeed train a dog, even a German Shorthaired Pointer!

Lastly, remember to view the situation from a different perspective. An energetic and intelligent dog like a German Shorthaired Pointer can indeed be more responsive to training. Their inbuilt drive to work and their intelligence can make training interesting and rewarding.

Therefore, by questioning your belief, looking at your past successes and adopting a different perspective, you can replace a limiting belief with a more inspiring one. This shift in mindset can open the door to an enriching and successful dog training experience.

You could go on to reframe your limiting beliefs into empowering ones. If you believe, "I'm not good enough to train a working dog", you might reframe it as "I have the ability to learn and improve as a dog trainer". This not only challenges your negative belief, but it also instils a positive mindset that encourages growth and development.

VISUALISING SUCCESS

One effective way to reinforce your new beliefs is through visualisation. Visualisation is a powerful tool that can help you change the way you think and behave. By vividly imagining your desired outcome — such as successfully training your dog — you can begin to believe in your ability to make it happen. Visualisation can also help you identify the steps you need to take to achieve your goal.

Start by finding a quiet, comfortable place where you won't be disturbed. Close your eyes and imagine yourself successfully training your dog. What do you see, hear and feel? Imagine the pride and satisfaction you would feel. Visualise the positive reactions from others. Let these images and feelings fill your mind and body.

Try to practice visualisation regularly. The more you do it, the stronger and more ingrained your new beliefs will become.

In addition to visualisation, affirmations also help you replace your limiting beliefs. Putting both together can be a winning formula. Repeat affirmations aloud to yourself, whilst visualising, especially when your limiting beliefs start to creep in.

Overcoming your limiting beliefs is critical as a dog trainer. Remember that growth and change take time and it's okay to make mistakes along the way. Be patient with yourself, celebrate your progress and remember to enjoy the progression with your dog. Overcoming your limiting beliefs is not just about becoming a better trainer, but also about growing as an individual.

VISUALISING YOUR INTENTIONS/GOALS: THE POWER OF VISION BOARDS

Vision boards can be powerful tools for motivation and visualisation. Essentially, a vision board is a visual representation of your intentions/goals, dreams, and aspirations. By physically laying out images, quotes and symbols that resonate with your hopes and desires, you make them more tangible and real. This can make your goals feel more attainable and real, encouraging you to work harder to achieve them.

When I first heard about vision boards, I found the idea a bit strange. Cutting out pictures and sticking them on a board seemed juvenile, like a primary school art project. I had my doubts, but decided to try it, keeping an open mind. Surprisingly, I found the activity deeply enjoyable and strangely therapeutic. It allowed me to dream freely and express my ambitions in a tangible form. Over time, I've grown to genuinely love my vision boards. It's a daily source of motivation, reminding me of my goals and what I'm working towards. It's gone from being a strange concept to an essential part of my success.

Creating a vision board can be fun and inspiring. You could include pictures of the things you want to achieve or the person you want to become. For instance, if you're training a dog to trial or compete, you might include images of well-trained, winning dogs, great trainers, places where you would love to compete and perhaps even your dream house and kennels with a spacious backyard for your many dogs. I know that's on my board but don't tell the husband!

In addition to images, vision boards can also include inspiring quotes, affirmations or words that resonate with your goals. These could be phrases like "I am a successful dog trainer" or "I am patient and understanding with my dog".

Once you've created your vision board, it's important to place it somewhere you can see it daily. This constant visual reminder of your goals can help to keep you focused and motivated, making your vision board a tool for both inspiration and accountability. Make it your computer screen saver or your mobile phone background.

Remember, the purpose of a vision board is to inspire and motivate, so there is no "right" or "wrong" way to make one. It should reflect your personal dreams and ambitions, designed in a way that appeals to you and brings you joy.

Over time, as you achieve your goals, you can update your vision board to reflect new aspirations. It can serve as a living testament to your growth and achievements, reminding you of how far you've come and where you're heading.

MASTERING DOG TRAINING: THE THREE DS AND THREE CS

Dog training sessions can be made simpler by focusing on three main aspects: Distance, Duration and Distraction. The Three Ds, as they're fondly known, provide a structured approach to gradually introducing your dog to different training scenarios. We teach about this in-depth in our flagship Hot Mess Handler course.

Distance: It's not just about the physical space between you and your dog or between your dog and a desired object. Distance represents the comfort zone. Too close to a distraction, and a dog might get overwhelmed. Too far from you, and they might feel isolated. Striking the right balance and adjusting your behaviour based on your dog's reactions is key.

Duration: This speaks about time. It's about how long your dog can maintain focus on a task or cue. By gradually increasing the duration of exercises, you're building your dog's endurance, both mentally and physically.

Distraction: The world is full of distractions, from squirrels running up trees to the smell of a nearby barbecue. Identifying and controlling these distractions will allow your dog to focus on tasks, even in challenging environments.

In this book, I won't talk about the Three Ds, as I leave this to the LWDG Group Experts, but I'd like to talk about the three Cs.

In this book, we've explored the Three Cs of Connection, Consistency and Confidence. Each principle holds transformative power in your dog training. When harmoniously combined, they create a dog trainer trifecta that's hard to rival.

This leads me to the concept of the Three Cs, designed not just as an educational tool but also as a memorable framework, akin to the established Three Ds.

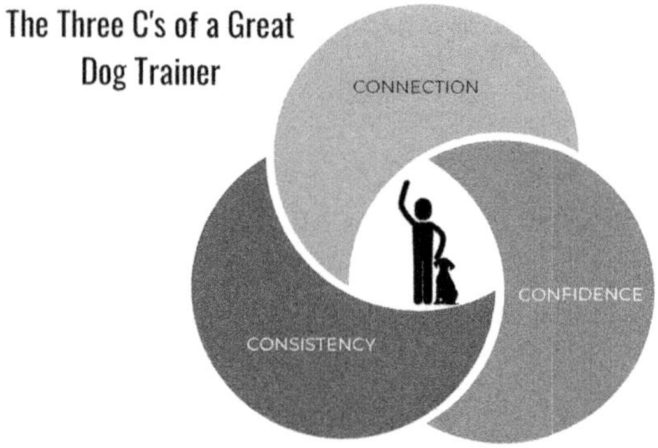

The beauty of the Three Cs is not merely in the principles they represent, but also in the simplicity with which they can be recalled. As trainers and devoted dog owners, amidst the whirlwind of daily tasks and distractions, it's important to have a concise, easily accessible reminder of your core training ethos. The Three Cs serve as that essential anchor.

While the Three Ds act as tangible, adjustable parameters in dog training, the Three Cs — Connection, Consistency and Confidence — acknowledge the complex dynamics of the relationship between you and your dog. These core principles are the heart and soul of effective training.

Connection: The Lifeline of Trust

Connection is not merely about familiarity but is deeply rooted in mutual trust and understanding. This shared bond is the cornerstone of all your training accomplishments.

Building Blocks of Connection:

- Time Together: Like any profound relationship, it grows stronger with shared experiences, be it play, training or simply lounging.
- Understanding Signals: Mastery in training is as much about 'listening' to your dog as it is about instructing. Attuning to their body language and signals offers valuable insights.
- Shared Emotions: Moments of joy, fear or excitement are shared experiences that reinforce your bond.

Consistency: The Language of Clarity

Why it Matters: Imagine learning a language where the meanings of words change daily. For dogs, inconsistency feels similar. Dogs thrive on routine and clear expectations. Being consistent in commands, rewards, training and even tone of voice ensures that your dog won't be second-guessing what's expected. It streamlines their learning process and reduces potential confusion.

Building Blocks of Consistency:

- Uniform Commands: A command should always solicit the same response, and maintaining command uniformity eliminates confusion.

- Rewards System: Rewarding desired behaviour should be systematic, ensuring the dog understands why they're being praised.
- Tone and Behaviour: Beyond words, dogs are keen observers of our tone and actions. Keeping them consistent cultivates better understanding.

Confidence: The Beacon in the Fog

In the vast world of scents, sights and sounds, your dog looks up to you as the guide. Your confidence is the beacon they follow.

Building Blocks of Confidence:

- Facing the Unknown: When confronted with unfamiliar situations, showing confidence reassures your dog, helping them navigate with trust.
- Internal Trust: Believe in the methods you've adopted and the potential of your dog. This inner confidence radiates outward.
- Handling Setbacks: Training isn't without setbacks. Approach them with constructive confidence, treating them as learning opportunities.

While you might be inclined to weigh the importance of the three Ds against the Three Cs, the essence of successful dog training lies in their intertwined application. Visualise the Three Ds as the framework of a house, giving shape and structure, while the Three Cs lay the strong foundation, ensuring the entire structure stands firm and resilient.

CHAPTER SNAPSHOT:

"Limiting beliefs" are thoughts that stop us from doing our best. For instance, feeling unsure about being able to train your dog.

- It's important to understand your thoughts and actions through self-reflection, to identify these beliefs.
- These beliefs often come from past experiences or societal expectations. They can affect how we behave and interact, including in our relationships with our dogs.
- To overcome these beliefs, start by questioning their truth. Remember your past successes and try to see things from a different perspective.
- Try changing negative thoughts into positive ones. For example, instead of thinking "I'm not good enough to train a dog," tell yourself, "I can learn and get better at training a dog".
- Using "visualisation" or picturing in your mind how you want things to go can help make these positive beliefs stronger.
- Make a vision board to help you build motivation and confidence and start to break down those limiting beliefs.
- Working through these beliefs isn't about becoming a better dog trainer. It's also about growing as a person and strengthening your bond with your dog. Remember to be patient with yourself, celebrate your progress and enjoy your time with your best friend.

READER EXERCISES

1. Identify a limiting belief you have about yourself as a dog owner and write down evidence to the contrary.
2. Create a vision board or collage that represents your aspirations as a dog owner and use it as a reminder of your potential.

FINAL THOUGHTS...

At the heart of this chapter, I hope you've appreciated that your journey with your dog goes beyond simple commands or routines. It's deeply intertwined with your personal growth and the narratives you tell yourself. Unpacking and challenging your limiting beliefs allows you to not only become a better trainer but also to grow closer and form a more authentic connection with your dogs. Remember, it's okay to be vulnerable, to confront those nagging doubts, and to rewrite the story you tell yourself. As you move forward, carry with you the knowledge, exercises and techniques from this chapter, but most importantly, carry the understanding that both you and your dog are on a continuous journey of growth and discovery together.

Middleton, A. (2022). *The Wall*. HarperCollins.

CHAPTER 10
YOUR PERSONALITY AND LEARNING STYLE

In 2006, I embarked on a journey to become a MAPS+ Facilitator through JCA Occupational Psychologists. This experience equipped me with a valuable tool to help my clients delve into their personalities, including their abilities, emotional intelligence, attitude and self-esteem, utilising the Myers-Briggs Type Indicator.

The Myers-Briggs Type Indicator, often abbreviated as MBTI, is a tool used to understand and categorise different personality types. It's designed to help individuals gain insights into their own behaviours, preferences and ways of interacting with the world around them.

Imagine you're in a room with a group of people. Each person has a unique way of approaching situations, making decisions and communicating with others. The MBTI aims to make sense of these differences by sorting people into specific personality types based on their tendencies and preferences.

The indicator is built upon four pairs of traits, each representing a different aspect of personality:

- ***Extroversion (E) vs. Introversion (I):*** This pair explores how people recharge and interact. Extroverts tend to be outgoing and social and gain energy from interactions with others. Introverts, on the other hand, are often more reserved, preferring quieter settings and needing alone time to recharge.

• ***Sensing (S) vs. Intuition (N):*** This pair focuses on how individuals gather information. People with a preference for Sensing rely on concrete facts and details, while those leaning towards Intuition are more inclined to see patterns and possibilities beyond the surface.

•***Thinking (T) vs. Feeling (F):*** This pair reflects how people make decisions. Thinkers tend to be analytical and logical, making choices based on objective reasoning. Feelers, in contrast, make decisions based on their values and consider the emotional impact on themselves and others.

•***Judging (J) vs. Perceiving (P):*** This pair deals with how people approach the outside world. Those with a Judging preference prefer structure, organization and clear plans. Perceivers are more adaptable, open to possibilities and tend to be spontaneous.

By combining these four pairs of traits, the MBTI generates sixteen distinct personality types, each represented by a four-letter code (e.g., ISTJ, ENFP, INFJ). These types serve as a way to describe certain consistent patterns in how individuals think, feel and behave.

It's important to note that the MBTI is a tool for self-discovery and can offer valuable insights into one's preferences and tendencies, however, it's not meant to be a definitive measure of personality and should be taken as a general framework rather than a strict classification. People can exhibit traits from both ends of each pair, and personalities can change and develop over time.

You can take the Myers-Briggs Type Indicator (MBTI) test for free on several websites. Keep in mind that while these free tests can give you an idea of your potential personality type, they might not be as comprehensive or accurate as the official MBTI assessment administered by certified professionals. Here are a few websites where you can take the test, 16Personalities is a website that, at the time of writing, offers a version of the MBTI test and provides detailed descriptions of each personality type. (Website: www.16personalities.com). You can also search online for 'Myers-Briggs Assessment' if you would like to explore your own personality type further.

Understanding the Myers-Briggs Type Indicator and its connection to your personality traits can notably enhance your approach to training working dogs. By recognising your type, you can tailor your training methods to your natural inclinations, making the process more effective and enjoyable.

Some trainers are naturally more outgoing and social **(Extroverts)**, while others are quieter and introspective **(Introverts).** The way you recharge and interact with the world shapes your training methods. Extroverts thrive in group settings, easily sharing ideas and collaborating with fellow trainers. Introverts, on the other hand, prefer quieter environments, paying close attention to subtle cues from their dogs during one-on-one sessions. When it comes to gathering information for training, think about two ways people do it: through facts and details **(Sensing)** or by recognising patterns and possibilities **(Intuition).** Sensing trainers prefer concrete information and practical techniques. They break down training into clear, step-by-step plans. Intuitive trainers, however, are more open to creative methods and can adapt their approach based on underlying patterns in their dogs' behaviour. Making decisions during training involves two distinct approaches: using logic and analysis **(Thinking)** or considering emotions and values **(Feeling).** Thinkers design training plans based on logical steps and measurable outcomes. Feelers, though, prioritise the emotional connection with their dogs, considering their feelings and building a strong bond. Lastly, consider how trainers deal with the structure of training: some prefer well-defined plans **(Judging)**, while others are more flexible and adaptable **(Perceiving)**. Judging trainers thrive on routines and schedules, planning each training session meticulously. Perceiving trainers, in contrast, embrace spontaneity and adjust their methods as needed, accommodating their dogs' responses and needs. Remember, most people are a mix of these traits. Understanding your tendencies can help you tailor your training style to match your strengths and effectively guide your working dogs.

Beyond the immediate training techniques, your personality type can influence various other aspects of the training process, creating a comprehensive impact on your interactions with working dogs:

Communication Style: Your personality type can shape how you communicate with your dogs. Extroverted trainers might use enthusiastic and outwardly expressive cues, while introverted trainers might employ subtler signals that resonate in one-on-one settings.

Training Environment: The training environment you prefer could be influenced by your personality. Extroverted trainers might enjoy bustling training centres with group activities, while introverted trainers might lean towards quieter, more controlled settings.

Stress Management: How you handle stress can impact your dogs. Extroverts might be good at maintaining a positive atmosphere during challenging training moments, while introverts might focus on maintaining a calm and composed attitude.

Training Goals: Your personality can influence the goals you set for your dogs. Thinkers might prioritise specific skills and achievements, while feelers might focus heavily on emotional well-being and the overall relationship.

Rewarding Approach: Your approach to rewarding your dog can be influenced by your personality traits. Thinkers, for instance, might prefer a systematic and consistent approach to doling out rewards, ensuring that they are closely tied to specific behaviours or achievements. Feelers, on the other hand, might emphasise emotional rewards, such as praise, petting and affection, creating a strong bond and a sense of joy during training sessions.

Training Plan Flexibility: Your adaptability in modifying training plans could be influenced by your personality. Perceiving trainers might easily adjust methods based on their dogs' responses, while judging trainers might prefer adhering to a predetermined plan, struggling if they need to adapt.

Innovative Techniques: Your willingness to experiment with new training methods might be tied to your personality type. Intuitive trainers could be more open to trying innovative approaches, while sensing trainers might prefer sticking to proven methods.

Teaching Methods: If you're able to teach others about dog training, your personality could influence your teaching style. Extroverts might enjoy dynamic, interactive workshops, while introverts might opt for more focused, detailed instruction.

Consistency: Your ability to maintain consistent training practices might vary based on your personality type. Judging trainers might excel in maintaining structured routines, while perceiving trainers might adapt their methods more readily.

Adapting to Different Dogs: Your adaptability in working with different dog personalities could be impacted by your own traits. Some trainers might naturally connect better with specific dog personalities that align with their own traits.

Problem-Solving Approach: When faced with training challenges, your personality can influence your problem-solving methods. Thinkers might analyse situations logically, while feelers might consider emotional factors.

Empathy and Intuition: Your natural empathy and intuitive understanding of your dog's emotions could stem from your personality. Feelers might excel at spotting subtle emotional cues in their dogs.

Remember that these influences merely offer insights into tendencies that might affect your training approach. The key is to leverage your strengths, be aware of your inclinations and strive for a well-rounded and adaptable training strategy that meets the diverse needs of your working dogs.

LEARNING STYLES

Understanding the interplay between personality types and learning styles can have a profound impact on your approach to dog training. Think of it as discovering how puzzle pieces fit together, each piece representing a unique trait, a specific teaching method and a stronger bond between you and your dog. As we explore this interaction, you'll gain insights into how it shapes your mindset.

Effective communication centres on understanding individual learning styles. VAK learning styles refer to a theory that classifies individuals into three primary learning preferences: Visual, Auditory and Kinaesthetic. These preferences represent the ways in which people tend to absorb and process information most effectively. Understanding VAK learning styles can help you tailor your learning preferences, enhancing your learning experience.

The VAK learning styles were conceptualised by Walter Burke Barbe and further developed by Neil Fleming. This learning model categorises individuals into three distinct learner types:

Visual Learners: Visual learners learn best through visual stimuli. They rely on seeing images, diagrams, charts and other visual aids to understand and retain information. Visual learners are often drawn to colourful presentations, videos and illustrations. They benefit from visual cues that help them organize and remember details.

Auditory Learners: Auditory learners excel when information is presented through sound and speech. They prefer listening to lectures, discussions and explanations. Auditory learners are skilled at retaining information through verbal instructions, discussions and audio materials. They might benefit from reciting information aloud or engaging in group discussions.

Kinaesthetic Learners: Kinaesthetic learners thrive when they can engage in hands-on, physical activities. They learn best by doing and experiencing. Kinaesthetic learners often prefer interactive activities, experiments, role-playing and practical applications of concepts. They may benefit from physically manipulating objects or participating in interactive exercises.

It's important to note that most individuals have a combination of these learning styles, with one style usually being more dominant. Additionally, you may have preferences that vary depending on the subject matter or context. While the concept of VAK learning styles has gained attention in educational settings, it's just one of many models used to understand individual learning preferences. As an owner training your dog, the concept of VAK Learning Styles can significantly contribute to your journey. By understanding and applying this concept, you can tailor your teaching approach to align with your own learning style, leading to better communication and more successful training.

If you're a visual learner, you can benefit immensely from watching videos and demonstrations of dog training techniques. Books and online resources with diagrams, infographics and pictorial guides about dog behaviour and training strategies can be particularly beneficial. Observing real-life training sessions or attending workshops can also provide you with visual insights into the process. Before attempting to train your dog, immerse yourself in visual resources to understand the nuances of dog training.

If auditory learning is your strength, consider listening to podcasts, audiobooks or seminars on dog training. Engage in discussions with seasoned dog trainers or join forums where training techniques are discussed. The clarity you receive from listening to explanations, stories and feedback can prepare you to articulate commands effectively and understand the importance of tone and pitch when training your dog.

If you're someone who learns best by doing, consider joining hands-on dog training workshops or apprentice under an experienced dog trainer. Engaging in real-life practice scenarios can provide invaluable experience. The tactile feedback from handling dogs in controlled environments can give you the confidence and skill set needed for successful training sessions.

By ensuring you're equipped with the right knowledge and skills, tailored to your learning preference, you pave the way for a more successful and enriching training experience for both you and your dog.

UNDERSTANDING YOUR OWN PERSONALITY AND LEARNING STYLES

You're a complex being, woven from intricate threads of perception and behaviour. Have you ever stopped to think about where you fit in this vast spectrum? Are you predominantly logical in your approach, or do emotions guide your decisions? When you're absorbing information, do visuals hold your attention, or are you swayed more by sounds or touch? It's a fascinating journey of self-discovery, and there are self-assessment tools available that can act as a guide, helping you unearth your unique training style. Once you have this insight, you'll find yourself better equipped to hone and adapt your techniques for optimum outcomes.

While understanding your personal tendencies is a strong start, it's your ability to adapt that can truly set you apart. Imagine you could combine the precise and methodical thinking you possess with an added layer of sensitivity and warmth. By doing this, you'll not only provide clear, structured guidance but also connect on an emotional level. What's more, if you're someone who typically makes decisions swiftly, consider occasionally stepping into the shoes of someone more spontaneous and you might discover innovative solutions to problems you face. Training is an art form, and you have the potential to be the maestro. By identifying and valuing the diversity in personalities and learning preferences, including your own, you can create a dynamic and versatile training approach. This is particularly essential if you're working with dogs, as each one is unique in temperament and learning style. As you navigate this intricate dance of personalities and methods, remember that your unwavering commitment and dedication are what will truly set you apart.

CHAPTER SNAPSHOT:

- Take an MBTI test and a VAK learning styles questionnaire online.
- For a week, maintain a diary of your training experiences. Analyse your MBTI and VAK influences.
- Choose a dog training topic you're unfamiliar with. Depending on your VAK result: Create an infographic (Visual), record a summary (Auditory), or perform a live demo (Kinaesthetic). After a day, review the learning aid and assess its effectiveness.

FINAL THOUGHTS...

Understanding different personalities and learning styles might seem like a tall order at first, but at its heart, it's really about tuning in to your natural inclinations and shaping your methods around them. The MBTI gives us a window into the intricate maze of human behaviour, showing us that we each have our own special way of seeing and reacting to the world. Just as the VAK learning styles remind us that learning is a deeply personal journey, not a one-size-fits-all process.

Training is truly about two things: communication and connection.

Getting to know our unique styles helps us communicate better, not just with people but with our dogs too. It's all about building a relationship where both trainer and dog feel understood and valued. And while tools like MBTI and VAK offer great insights, they're just the beginning. The real transformation comes when we blend this knowledge with kindness, understanding and true affection for both us and our dogs.

CHAPTER 11
INTENTIONS, INTUITION AND TRUST

Let's be honest, at the beginning of this book you probably felt like you were in over your head. Maybe you're new to the world of dog training, or you're struggling with a particularly challenging dog. Maybe you're dealing with self-doubt or imposter syndrome, wondering if you're really cut out for this. It's understandable to feel this way, but hopefully now, after reading this book you know that you are capable, competent and deserving of success.

In the world of dog training, one of the biggest obstacles can come from within - self-sabotage. Self-sabotage is when we knowingly or unknowingly destroy our own efforts, preventing us from reaching our goals or fulfilling our potential. It can stem from various sources, including fear of failure, fear of success or a deep-seated belief that we don't deserve to succeed.

UNDERSTANDING SELF-SABOTAGE

Self-sabotage can manifest in many ways in dog training. Maybe you procrastinate on training sessions, telling yourself that you're too busy or too tired and that you'll do it tomorrow. Perhaps you consistently set unrealistic expectations for yourself and your dog, only to feel deflated when they aren't met. Or you might find yourself in a cycle of negative self-talk, convincing yourself that you're not capable, or that your dog would be better off with another handler.

Recognising these patterns of self-sabotage is the first step towards overcoming them. It can be helpful to journal about your thoughts and feelings around training, to identify any recurring themes or patterns. You might find that your self-sabotage stems from a fear of failure or an ingrained belief that you aren't capable or deserving of success, as we discussed in the previous chapter.

Writing this book has had its fair share of sabotage storms. There were moments of self-doubt and self-sabotage when I nearly surrendered to the belief that I couldn't possibly complete this book. I nearly gave up, allowing my own fears and doubts to cast a shadow on my passion to do this. Self-sabotage can be conquered in one area of your life, only to show up somewhere else as you expand outside your comfort zone.

RECOGNISING SELF-SABOTAGE

Looking back, I can clearly see the signs of self-sabotage. I found myself procrastinating, repeatedly pushing back my writing schedule, reasoning that I was too tired, not inspired enough, or simply didn't have the time. I convinced myself that the book wouldn't be good enough, that no one would read it or that I didn't have anything significant to say. I told myself that no one could ever expect me to do this in the timescale I had, with everything else going on, and everyone would understand if I didn't complete it. I also set unrealistically high expectations for myself, striving for perfection in every sentence and paragraph, only to end up disappointed when I fell short. Each time I read what I'd written, I hated it, and I still do sometimes. After all, who am I to author a book, train a gundog, or run the LWDG?

The consequence of these self-defeating thoughts and actions was a heavy feeling of disheartenment. I felt stuck, as though I was in a constant battle against myself. It was an emotionally draining experience that left me feeling defeated. There were days I believed I was destined to fail, that this book was beyond my capabilities. I was on the brink of giving up, ready to let go of the dream I had nurtured for so long.

CHANGING MY THOUGHT PROCESS

But then, I took a big step back. I allowed myself to breathe, to reflect, to understand where this self-sabotage was coming from. I began to understand that my fears of failure, of not being good enough, were the fuel to this self-sabotage. I made the decision to turn this stinking thinking around. I started by acknowledging my negative thoughts and then actively worked to replace them with positive affirmations. I reminded myself of my passion for gundogs and my desire to share my knowledge and experiences with my community. I began to believe in the value of my story, and the unique insights I could offer.

I also sought support from my peers, those who had been through similar experiences. I was humbled to find that self-doubt and self-sabotage were common occurrences, even among seasoned authors. Knowing that I was not alone in this struggle gave me strength and the confidence to keep going. I reminded myself that writing a book is hard, it's not meant to be easy. It's about learning, growing and sharing, not achieving perfection. I set more realistic expectations for myself, learned to appreciate the progress I was making and started celebrating small victories, like finishing a chapter or thinking of something that would improve it.

And so, I continued. Each day, I showed up for myself. I wrote, edited, reviewed and rewrote. There were still days of struggle, but now I had tools to combat my self-sabotage. The understanding and acceptance of my self-sabotage was liberating. It allowed me to step out of my own way and let my love for gundogs and the expertise and experiences I wanted to share take the forefront.

I won't pretend it was easy, but it was rewarding. Writing this book and overcoming the self-sabotage that almost halted its creation, was another personal triumph. I am constantly reminded that the most significant barriers we face are often the ones we place before ourselves, and overcoming those barriers begins with acknowledging their existence.

I am immensely proud of this book, not just for the content it carries, but for the personal growth and learning that happened behind the scenes. I hope that by sharing my experience of writing what you are reading, you can recognise and overcome your own self-sabotage, whether it's in training your dog or in any other endeavour you embark on. Remember, the only limit to your success is you.

CONQUER YOUR INNER BATTLES, AND YOU'LL BE UNSTOPPABLE

It's easy to feel like you're not good enough, especially when you're comparing yourself to others or facing obstacles in your training, but the truth is, you have a unique set of skills, experiences and strengths that make you an excellent dog owner. As a dog owner, you have a special bond with **YOUR** dog that allows you to communicate in ways that are beyond words. The bond between a dog and their owner is truly unique. It's a connection that goes beyond words and is based on mutual trust, love, understanding and your time together.

It's easy to focus on the negatives and feel like you're not making progress, but it's important to take a step back and recognise your unique qualities and strengths. For instance, maybe you have a natural talent for reading your dog's body language and responding to their needs. This could be a valuable skill when it comes to training and handling your dog, and you should recognise it as a strength. Or perhaps you have a lot of patience and persistence, which can be essential when working with a challenging dog. By recognising and celebrating these qualities, you can build a stronger sense of self-worth and confidence in your abilities.

IMPOSTER SYNDROME

It's normal to feel like you don't know what you're doing sometimes. You may experience self-doubt or wonder if you're cut out for this. It's easy to fall into the trap of thinking you're not good enough. Maybe you compare yourself to other dog owners and feel like you're not measuring up, or you're dealing with imposter syndrome and feel like you're pretending to be something you're not.

No one knows everything there is to know about dog ownership, there's always room for improvement. By improving your skills and knowledge, you can feel more confident in your ability to handle any hurdles that come your way. But you can only do this by acting on it.

Try reframing your self-talk to focus on your strengths and accomplishments. For example, instead of thinking "I'm not good enough to train my dog," try thinking "I may have some areas to work on, but I've already made progress and I'm capable of learning and growing". By focusing on the positives and recognising your achievements, you can build confidence and self-belief.

LEARNING FROM MISTAKES AND FAILURES

Nobody's perfect and everyone makes mistakes. As a dog owner, it's important to acknowledge that failures and mistakes are a natural part of the learning process. Instead of beating yourself up over them, try to learn from them.

Reflect on what went wrong and why and think about how you can do better next time. This can help you build resilience and adaptability, which are essential qualities for any dog owner.

TRUSTING YOUR INSTINCTS

As individuals, we often face moments that require quick thinking and adaptation. This is where trusting your intuition comes in. Your instincts can help you identify when something is not right or when you need to make a change. For instance, if you feel like your dog is not progressing in their training, or if you feel like a certain training method is not working, you should trust your instincts and adjust as needed. When you start to trust your intuition, you'll become more confident in your decision-making and in your ability to work with your dog.

Developing your intuition takes practice, but it's a skill that will develop with time and effort. One way to start is by paying close attention to your own feelings and reactions in different situations. By paying attention to these cues, you can adjust your approach accordingly and make better decisions. Trusting your instincts doesn't mean ignoring knowledge or experience. Rather, it's about using all the tools at your disposal to make informed decisions. When you combine your intuition with both your knowledge and experience, you'll be better equipped to handle whatever comes your way. Trusting your instincts means paying attention to your dog's body language, behaviour, and needs. Developing this skill takes practice, but it can be done with time and effort. One way to start is by paying close attention to your dog's body language during training sessions. Take, for example, if your dog is becoming frustrated or tired, they may start to exhibit certain signs such as panting, showing off or avoiding eye contact. By acknowledging and reacting to these cues, you can adjust your training methods accordingly. Practising being present in the moment during training sessions can also help you develop your intuition as you will be far more observant.

Trusting your instincts can also help you build confidence in yourself and your dog. When you start to acknowledge and react immediately to your dog's needs and respond to them intuitively, you'll feel more in control of the situation. This confidence can lead to greater success in training and working together. The ability to learn from the past, trust your instincts, and intuition and pull on your confidence is central to your success as a handler.

UNDERSTANDING YOUR DOG'S NEEDS

Working dogs have specific needs and requirements that differ from those of companion dogs. They need to be physically fit AND mentally stimulated. Understanding and meeting these needs is critical to your success as a handler. When you understand your dog's needs, you can create a more fulfilling training and working relationship. You'll be able to provide the physical and mental stimulation that your dog requires, and you'll be able to recognise when your dog is overworked or in need of rest.

CHAPTER SNAPSHOT:

- Identify negative self-talk and replace it with positive affirmations. Instead of focusing on your weaknesses, acknowledge your unique strengths and accomplishments.
- Practice mindfulness during training sessions to become more attuned to your dog's needs and body language. By paying attention to subtle cues, you can adjust your training methods and create a stronger working relationship with your dog.
- Learn from failures and mistakes. Instead of beating yourself up over setbacks, reflect on what went wrong and

think about how you can do better next time. This can help you build resilience and adaptability as a dog owner.

- Trust your instincts and intuition. By paying attention to your own feelings and reactions, you can make informed decisions and adjust your approach accordingly. Combine your intuition with knowledge and experience to become a more confident and capable handler.
- Focus on building a strong bond with your dog. By understanding their unique personality and needs, you can create a deeper, more meaningful relationship that is based on mutual trust and respect. This bond can also provide emotional support during challenging times.

READER EXERCISES

1. Take a moment to identify any behaviours or thoughts you've been harbouring that could be seen as self-sabotaging. This might include actions like repeatedly putting off tasks, or thoughts that undermine your confidence, such as telling yourself you're not capable enough. Write these behaviours and thoughts down in a list.
2. Write down a negative thought you frequently have about yourself or your abilities. This could be something like "I'm not good at training dogs" or "I can't handle this". Now, challenge this thought. Write down three solid reasons why this negative thought isn't true.
3. Keep a 'Self-Sabotage Journal' for a week, or longer if you wish. In this journal, note down instances where you've noticed yourself procrastinating, being overly critical of yourself, or setting unrealistic expectations. At the end of the week, review your entries and look for patterns. What self-sabotaging behaviours show up the most?

4. Identify a time when you trusted your instincts as a dog owner and reflect on the positive outcomes that resulted.
5. Write a letter of gratitude to your dog, acknowledging the strengths and skills you've developed because of your relationship.

FINAL THOUGHTS...

As this chapter wraps up, I want to remind you of the importance of trust. Trust in your dog and, more importantly, trust in yourself. It's okay to make mistakes; they're just part of the learning process. Listen to your dog, but also listen to your own heart and gut feelings. Together, you and your dog will grow and succeed. Remember, you've got this, and your dog believes in you just as much as I do.

CHAPTER 12
KEEP YOURSELF IN THE EQUATION

Amid all the challenging dog training you do, it's easy to forget about the most important element in the equation: **YOU**. That's right - this chapter is all about why taking care of yourself is just as important as taking care of your four-legged friend. I'm going to dive into why prioritising your own well-being is essential for success as a working dog owner.

From boosting your own happiness to strengthening your relationship with your dog, I want to talk to you about all the ways that self-care can make a difference and how to keep yourself in the equation, so that you and your dog can thrive.

YOU ARE IMPORTANT

It's natural to pour all your attention into your dog's needs, but don't forget, you are just as essential to this equation as your dog. Without your hard work and dedication, your dog's training and progress wouldn't be possible.

That's why taking care of yourself is just as important as taking care of your dog. In fact, prioritising your own well-being can have numerous benefits for both you and your four-legged friend such as:

More energy: When you invest in self-care, you'll have more energy to devote to training and caring for your dog. With increased focus and enthusiasm, you'll be able to handle the demands of training and your dog will benefit from your renewed sense of purpose.

Better focus: We all know that stress and overwhelm can make it hard to concentrate. By prioritising self-care, you'll enhance your capability to manage anxiety and stay focused during training sessions. This can lead to more efficient and effective training, benefiting both you and your dog.

Less stress: By taking care of yourself, you can reduce overall stress levels and feel more balanced and grounded. This can improve your own mental health.

Stronger bond: When you're in a positive state of mind, you'll be more attuned to your dog's needs and able to communicate more effectively. A happy, healthy owner often means a happy, healthy dog.

HOW TO PRIORITISE YOUR WELL-BEING

Now that we've established the importance of self-care, let's discuss some practical ways to improve your physical, mental and emotional well-being.

Physical activity is indispensable for maintaining your health and well-being. Engaging in regular exercise can help improve your mood, reduce stress and increase your energy levels. By participating in activities such as walking, running, swimming or any other form of exercise that you enjoy, you're making a conscious effort to look after yourself. Many forms of exercise can be combined with your dog's daily activities, such as walking, which creates a fun and healthy experience that you both can enjoy. But also take time to do things away from your dog so that you have space where you aren't having to worry about their behaviour or obedience.

Getting enough sleep is vital for your overall health and well-being. A good night's sleep allows your body to recharge and recover from the demands of your day. It's essential to ensure you're getting sufficient rest each night to function optimally during your training sessions and daily tasks. A well-rested owner is more likely to be focused, patient and better equipped to handle a dog training session.

A balanced diet plays a significant role in your physical and mental health. By fuelling your body with the right nutrients, you're ensuring that you have the energy and focus required to care for your working dog. Eating well not only improves your physical health, but it can also positively impact your mental well-being by stabilising your mood and increasing your energy levels. Making good nutrition a priority means making healthier choices and paying attention to your body's needs. Just as you know poor nutrition can affect your dog's behaviour, it affects yours too. You go out of your way to choose the best nutrition for your dog, so do the same for yourself, too.

Staying connected with friends, family, or other owners is essential for your emotional well-being. Sharing experiences, seeking advice and learning from others can provide valuable support and encouragement. By maintaining these social connections, you're fostering a sense of belonging and building a network of individuals who understand the unique difficulties and joys of working dog ownership. It's also important not to lose all your non-dog friends. Going for a meal or to the cinema where your dog isn't discussed is not a bad thing. It will give you a break.

Another great way to take care of yourself is to know when to say "no". Setting boundaries is essential for maintaining balance in your life. By setting limits on your commitments and responsibilities, you can prevent burnout and ensure you have time for self-care. Establishing boundaries helps you focus on your well-being, allowing you to concentrate on the tasks and activities that truly matter.

Cultivating mindfulness through practices such as meditation, yoga or deep breathing exercises can help you stay present and focused. These practices can reduce stress, improve your mental well-being and enhance your overall quality of life. By valuing mindfulness, you're better able to manage the stress and demands of working dog ownership with grace and resilience.

Engaging in activities you enjoy outside of working with your dog can provide a sense of accomplishment, joy and relaxation. Hobbies can offer a much-needed break from the demands of working dog ownership, allowing you to recharge and maintain a sense of balance. By pursuing hobbies and interests, you're focusing on your well-being and investing in your happiness. Piano and sugar craft both make a huge difference for me, and they improve my dog training by allowing my mind to switch off and then come back at the problem rested.

SEEKING PROFESSIONAL HELP

If you're struggling with your mental or emotional health, it's important to consider seeking professional help from a therapist or counsellor. These mental health professionals can provide valuable guidance and support as you plough through life's challenges. Looking after your mental health is a crucial aspect of overall well-being and you must look after yourself before you look after training. Never be scared to step away and take a break. No dog was ruined for life by missing a few weeks of training.

RECOGNISING THE SIGNS OF BURNOUT AND SEEKING HELP WHEN NEEDED

I briefly discussed burnout earlier in this book, however, I want to talk about it more here as it's essential to recognise the signs of burnout. Early detection can prevent long-term consequences and help you maintain your well-being.

Juggling many things at once really took a toll on me this year. Between working my dogs, running the LWDG, dealing with my brain tumour, moving home, helping Charlotte, my daughter, move home, and still, nearly four years in, learning to cope with the loss of my dad, I ended up feeling incredibly unwell. All the stress from training, a busy family life and supporting other dog owners, on top of my own personal health problems, pushed me to my limits. My health went further downhill, and I just didn't feel the same passion for dog training anymore.

Luckily, my friends saw what was happening and stepped in to help. They made me realise how important it was to take a step back and focus on my own well-being. Even with my own knowledge and experience, I was ignoring the tell-tale signs.

With their support, I started to reprioritise, and I began to focus more on self-care. By adjusting my expectations, I was able to get back on track with my health and find my love for working with dogs again.

SOME COMMON SIGNS OF BURNOUT

Physical symptoms: Constant fatigue, frequent illnesses, headaches and muscle pain can be indicators of burnout. When your body is consistently under stress, your immune system can become compromised, making you more susceptible to illness.

Emotional symptoms: Feelings of hopelessness, irritability, cynicism and detachment can signal burnout. These emotions may manifest as increased frustration with your dog, a lack of empathy or an overall negative outlook.

Reduced performance: A decline in motivation, productivity or focus during training sessions and daily tasks can be a sign that burnout is taking its toll. This may lead to difficulty concentrating, making decisions or remembering important details.

Changes in behaviour: Burnout can lead to noticeable changes in your behaviour, such as withdrawing from social activities, procrastinating or using unhealthy coping mechanisms like overeating, substance abuse or excessive screen time.

TACKLING BURNOUT

Experiencing burnout can be incredibly challenging, but it's important to remember that seeking help is a sign of strength and self-awareness. By taking proactive steps to address burnout, you're making well-being a top priority and setting yourself up for a healthier, more fulfilling life as a working dog owner.

One of the most crucial steps in overcoming burnout is leaning on your support network. Don't hesitate to reach out to friends, family or fellow working dog owners. Sharing your feelings with people who care about you can provide much-needed empathy, encouragement and practical advice.

Another essential element of combating burnout is putting self-care first. Carve out time for activities that help you relax and recharge, like exercise, hobbies or spending time in nature. Make sure you're getting enough sleep, eating well and practising mindfulness to nurture your overall well-being. Remember that taking care of yourself is just as important as taking care of your dog, and doing so will benefit both of you in the long run. Do all the things I've talked about earlier as ways of prevention as they also offer the cure.

Establishing healthy boundaries is also key in dealing with burnout. Take a close look at your commitments and responsibilities and learn to say "no" when necessary. By setting limits, you'll create a more manageable workload, reducing the risk of further burnout. It's essential to find a balance that allows you to maintain your passion for working with dogs while also preserving your own well-being.

I can't stress this enough. Don't be afraid to seek professional help if your burnout symptoms persist or worsen. There's no shame in seeking assistance and doing so can make a significant difference in your overall mental health.

Lastly, take a step back and re-evaluate your intentions, expectations and priorities in your life, including your role as a working dog owner. Adjust as needed to create a more balanced and sustainable lifestyle. This might involve redefining success or finding new ways to approach training and caring for your dog that better align with your personal needs and limitations. Always remember that your well-being is just as important as your dog's, and taking care of yourself is necessary for both your and your dog's success.

DOGGY BURNOUT

Dogs, much like their human counterparts, can also experience burnout through overtraining. As a trainer, it's essential to be mindful of our canine companions' needs and the importance of allowing them to take breaks as well. Overworking a dog can lead to physical and mental exhaustion, decreased enthusiasm and reduced performance in training sessions. It is crucial to strike a balance between maintaining a consistent training regimen and providing your dog with adequate rest and relaxation time.

By observing your dog's behaviour and energy levels, you can recognise when they need a break and give them the opportunity to recharge. Providing your dog with time to rest and engage in leisurely activities not only helps prevent burnout but also contributes to a stronger bond between you, resulting in a happier and healthier partnership.

CHAPTER SNAPSHOT:

- **You matter** in the dog training process.
- The benefits of self-care include more energy, better focus, less stress and a closer bond with your dog.
- Strategies for well-being include regular exercise, adequate sleep, a balanced diet, maintaining social connections, setting boundaries, practising mindfulness and pursuing hobbies.
- It's essential to seek professional mental health assistance when needed.
- Be aware of burnout signs such as physical symptoms, emotional changes and altered behaviours.
- To address burnout, lean on support networks, emphasise self-care, establish boundaries and adjust personal expectations.
- Dogs can also experience burnout, so monitor their well-being alongside your own.

READER EXERCISES

1. Create a self-care routine that includes activities that nourish your physical, emotional and mental well-being.
2. Write a list of warning signs that you may be experiencing burnout and create a plan for addressing them proactively.

FINAL THOUGHTS...

As you conclude this chapter, I want you to remember something fundamental. Sometimes, the best thing we can do is pause, take a deep breath and re-evaluate our approach. It's not just about the techniques or methods; it's about you at the core of this journey. This chapter is my heartfelt nudge to you, underscoring your indispensable role in this training process. Always prioritise your well-being. When you take care of yourself, it directly benefits your dog and those around you.

CHAPTER 13
THINGS OWNERS SAY TO THEMSELVES...

This section is what our community say the most, and what I say back. Can you identify yourself in any of these?

"I'm not good enough to train my dog."
My Answer: You are good enough! Dog training is a skill that can be learned. All it takes is patience, consistency, and a willingness to learn.

"I don't have enough time to train my dog properly."
My Answer: Training a dog doesn't always require huge blocks of time. Even a few minutes here and there throughout your day can make a big difference. Find the time, even if it's short.

"Training a dog is too hard; I can't do it."
My Answer: It might seem hard, especially at the start, but don't let that discourage you. Breaking down the training into smaller steps can make it more manageable.

"My dog's behaviour is out of control, and it's all my fault."
My Answer: It's not your fault, but it's your responsibility. Dogs don't behave badly to upset you; they simply don't understand what's expected. With consistent training and clear communication, you can guide your dog to better behaviour.

"I've never been able to train a dog before, so I won't be able to train this one."
My Answer: Past experiences don't dictate future outcomes. Use your past experience as a learning tool and remember that each dog is different.

"I don't have the skills to handle a working dog."
My Answer: You can develop those skills! There are many resources available to you such as groups like the LWDG, books, online videos and local trainers, all here to help you learn how to train a working dog.

"I'm not assertive enough to manage a dog, I have got to be mean, haven't I?"
My Answer: Being assertive doesn't mean being harsh or aggressive at all. It's about clear, consistent communication. You can learn to be assertive in a kind and effective way.

"My dog is too stubborn; he's untrainable."
My Answer: There are very few truly untrainable dogs, only unexplored training methods. Some dogs might require a different approach, but with patience and perseverance, all dogs can learn.

"I can't afford the training resources or professional help."
My Answer: There are many affordable or even free resources available, our website is full of them. Start with what you can manage, and remember, consistency and dedication often matter more than expensive tools or trainers.

"I am too old/young to train a dog properly."
My Answer: Age is not a barrier to dog training. Both young and old individuals have successfully trained dogs. What matters most is your willingness to learn and adapt to your dog's needs.

"My dog would behave better if it had a different owner."
My Answer: You are the perfect owner for your dog. You know your dog better than anyone else and can provide the love, guidance and consistency they need.

"I'm too nervous or anxious to train my dog effectively."
My Answer: It's okay to feel this way. Start with small steps and gradually increase your confidence. Training can actually be therapeutic and help to reduce anxiety over time.

"My dog is too old/young to learn new things."
My Answer: Dogs are never too old or too young to learn. Training methods may need to be adjusted for age, but learning can always occur.

"I don't have the patience to train a dog."
My Answer: Patience is something that can be developed over time. Take deep breaths, take breaks when needed, and remember to reward yourself for progress.

"I'm just not a 'dog person'."
My Answer: You don't have to identify as a 'dog person' to train a dog successfully. If you are dedicated and willing to understand your dog's needs, you are enough.

"My dog's bad behaviour is a reflection of my failures."
My Answer: Dogs are individuals with their own temperaments and behaviours. While training plays a role, a dog's behaviour is not a direct reflection of your worth or abilities.

"I should have known better, but I missed the signs."
My Answer: We all miss signs sometimes. What's important is to learn from these experiences and apply that knowledge moving forward.

"I'll never be able to train my dog as well as a professional."
My Answer: Professionals have years of experience, but that doesn't mean you can't achieve great results. Your relationship with your dog is unique and valuable in its own right.

"My dog will never be as well-behaved as other dogs."
My Answer: Every dog is unique, and comparison isn't helpful. Focus on the progress your dog is making, not on other dogs.

"It's too late to change my dog's behaviour now."
My Answer: It's never too late to teach an old dog new tricks. Change might take time, but with consistency, patience and love, your dog can learn new behaviours.

The reality is you are more capable than you give yourself credit for. With patience, dedication and a willingness to learn, you can build a wonderful bond with your dog and accomplish your training goals.

CHAPTER 14
WHAT'S NEXT

Through the pages of this book, you've found your way through the vast and complex world of working with dogs, covering everything from the importance of understanding your impact on your dog and the perils of over-criticism, to the highs and lows of the first year together. It has been a mission filled with insights, difficulties, successes and lessons.

As I close this book, it's my hope that you carry forward the lessons learned, applying them to your unique path with your own dog. Remember, the voyage is not always easy, but it is undoubtedly rewarding. There's no 'one-size-fits-all' approach to training your working dog, and that's the beauty of it. Every dog is unique, and every relationship between a handler and their dog is equally unique. One of the most fabulous things that the LWDG has given me is so many friendships with many different people, with varying backgrounds, places they call home and bank balances, but what unites them, their common ground, is their dogs. By having a dog, you have automatically qualified to enter our world and be part of our friendship.

Always be patient with your dog and, most importantly, with yourself. Be mindful of your thoughts and emotions, for they deeply influence your dog's behaviour. Celebrate the progress, no matter how small it may seem, for every step forward is a victory worth celebrating.

The following quote, by Jim Rohn, holds special meaning for me, particularly in the context of life and dog training.

> *"We must all suffer from one of two pains: the pain of discipline or the pain of regret. The difference is discipline weighs ounces while regret weighs tons."*

This speaks to the importance of early effort and dedication. In training dogs, spending time and effort at the beginning might seem tough, but it's worth it. If we skip or rush this early training, we may face challenges with our dog's behaviour later, leading to regret. Rohn's words remind me to always put in the necessary work now, so I don't look back with wishes of having done things differently. No matter how much you learn, there will always be another layer of complexity to uncover, another behaviour to understand, another strategy to master. This endless opportunity for growth is what makes dog training so fascinating and rewarding. Every new experience with your dog brings you a step closer to unlocking another level of understanding and communication with them.

As with many areas in life, the progression towards becoming an accomplished dog trainer is not a destination but an ongoing pathway of learning, discovery, growth and adaptation. This field is constantly evolving, shaped by new research, developing techniques and a deeper understanding of canine behaviour and communication. The constant evolution of this field is exciting, but it can also be overwhelming at times. Remember, nobody knows everything and even the most experienced trainers continue to learn and adapt their methods. It's okay to make mistakes and to not have all the answers. What's important is your willingness to learn from these experiences, to remain open to new information and methods, and to continually strive to improve your understanding and techniques.

Being a successful dog trainer requires patience, curiosity and an enduring commitment to learning. It's about learning to understand your dog, but it's also about understanding yourself, your reactions and your strategies. By continuing to learn, you're not only improving your skills and knowledge but also fostering a stronger and deeper union with your dog.

So, what does the future look like? It may mean seeking out new books, attending seminars, watching training videos or joining a local dog club. It may mean working with a mentor or hiring a coach to guide you in more advanced training methods. It hopefully also involves you joining us within the LWDG. And importantly, it involves a lot of hands-on experience with your dog. Every interaction with your dog is an opportunity to learn, to grow, and to become a better trainer.

As you continue this journey, stay curious, remain patient, and embrace the setbacks and rewards that come with learning. The road to becoming a successful dog trainer is a marathon, not a sprint. It's a journey that's filled with many steps, both forwards and sometimes backwards. But each step, each moment, brings you and your dog closer together and, ultimately, that's the most rewarding outcome of all. May the insights from this book guide you, inspire you, and serve as a beacon when times get tough. And remember, you're not alone. Whether it's our community, a trainer or fellow dog owners, support is always available. You just need to reach out.

Remember to savour every moment with your working dog, for these are the moments that make this adventure truly extraordinary. Here's to a successful, fulfilling and enriching journey with your working dog!

Much Love,
Jo xx

Visit
www.ladiesworkingdoggroup.com/tdt-resources
to download free resources.

Facebook
www.facebook.com/ladiesworkingdoggroup

Instagram
@ladiesworkingdogs

Podcast Platform
'Found It, Fetched It'

THE LADIES WORKING DOG GROUP

A Warm Welcome to the Ladies Working Dog Group

I'm excited to formally introduce you to a unique group that has etched an influential niche in the UK's working dog handlers' landscape - the Ladies Working Dog Group. Our passion goes beyond merely training our dogs. We strive to develop a supportive and safe environment for women across the world to join and support each other in this often challenging, yet incredibly rewarding pastime.

THE SPARK THAT LIT THE FLAME

Raised on a smallholding, I've always loved nature and animals, but my passion for working dogs was truly ignited during that first outing with my father. The profound connection between him and his dogs, their seemingly intuitive understanding of each other and their seamless teamwork was captivating. However, finding my place in this field wasn't easy as a woman. I experienced moments of exclusion from men who believed this realm was not meant for women. Their views, however, have only fuelled my determination. I must state here that these men were and are very much in the minority. Most men are fabulous to women in the sport, but there is a vocal minority who can make it an uncomfortable place to be - the rotten apples in the barrel, so to speak.

My personal journey began with me training with my father and receiving guidance from those kind-hearted individuals that were his friends, but I also wanted to find other women to talk to and I knew there had to be many more women like me — passionate about working dogs but experiencing feelings of isolation and a lack of support.

I knew they had to be out there, my daughter had been part of the picking-up team, aged fourteen, on the Glan Usk Estate with my dad - she'd even been to the Gamekeepers Class at Crufts! But as she got older, she stopped. I still ponder regularly how many young ladies start and leave the sport, and in the first few months, I wondered how many women there were that I could locate. That need to find them sparked the start of the Ladies Working Dog Group, an escape where women could support and uplift each other in a totally safe space.

Our initial members were the few women I met while out in the field right at the start, each with their unique trials and stories. Bound by our shared experiences and our love for our dogs, we embarked on group building together. In our early days as a Facebook group, we were named 'Women Beaters and Pickers Up'. Membership growth was slow and somewhat eventful, attracting interest from men whose intentions were 'at best' questionable. Our name quickly changed to suit the people we actually wanted to attract.

Now, many years on from just a Facebook Group, the true heart of the Ladies Working Dog Group lies in our LWDG Society Membership community. We strongly believe that no woman should need to figure out dog handling alone. We stand together, offering advice, sharing experiences, celebrating victories and learning from setbacks.

TRAINING TAILORED TO EACH DOG AND TO EACH OWNER

We place a strong emphasis on the individuality of each dog in our training approach. Recognising that no two dogs are alike, we believe in understanding and meeting our dogs' unique needs and personalities. After all, the key is to train the dog that stands before you.

Acknowledging the difficulties of juggling various roles —mother, wife, professional — alongside our responsibilities as dog trainers, we urge each other to find a balance that doesn't require abandoning our dog-related passions. We pool our collective wisdom to help each other excel in all areas of our lives. Continuous learning, flexibility and thorough training form a huge part of our membership.

The Ladies Working Dog Group remains connected and engaged through a load of activities and initiatives. Our bi-monthly live online coaching sessions and our in-person training meetings across the UK offer us opportunities to learn from each other and our dogs, improving our skills while deepening our friendships. These meetings form the backbone of our community.

THE UNIQUE PERSPECTIVE OF WOMEN IN DOG TRAINING

Public education and awareness are of importance to us. We seek to promote the rewarding aspects of working with dogs and highlight the vital role women can play in this sphere.

We also prioritise collaboration with other working dog organisations. Through making alliances, we exchange experiences, knowledge and resources, benefiting each other while furthering our commitment to a more extensive community.

The Ladies Working Dog Group has had a permanent impact on its members and the wider dog-handling community. We take pride in the mass of empowering stories that our members can share, having found confidence, camaraderie and purpose through their association with us. We have succeeded in improving the perception of women in the working dog sphere, proving that we can match our male counterparts.

Looking ahead, we acknowledge the old and new obstacles on our path. The COVID-19 pandemic compelled us to adapt and find novel ways to stay connected, offer support and continue our work, and those adaptations are welcomed in a sport where many of us must train alone. The advancements we made have turned our space into an incredible network where there are no boundaries and where isolation is unnecessary. We are steadfast in our commitment to ensure the growth and sustainability of our group.

In essence, the Ladies Working Dog Group is a haven, a family of women who are dedicated to their dogs and each other. We have come a long way, but our trek is far from over. We will continue to nurture, learn and grow, upholding the spirit of community and our love for working dogs.

HOW TO JOIN

If you are a woman with a passion for working dogs and are considering joining our vibrant community, we would be thrilled to welcome you onboard! The process is straightforward and can be completed entirely online. By visiting our website at www.ladiesworkingdoggroup.com, you can find all the information about our membership benefits. A few clicks will get you immediate access to our extensive resources.

As a member, you gain access to our trove of online training masterclasses. These courses cater to all experience levels, providing insights, tips and strategies to hone your skills as a working dog handler. You also gain access to the LWDG Society Private Podcast. This resource is a goldmine of knowledge, discussions, interviews and advice that cater to our shared passion.

Another perk of membership is access to our live coaching calls and a library of past coaching call recordings, a treasure chest of advice and solutions to issues common in working dog handling.

Beyond these educational resources, the core benefit of joining the Ladies Working Dog Group is the access to our supportive online community. This network is a space to connect with like-minded women, sharing your story along the way. It's a place to exchange experiences, ask questions, celebrate successes and find support during challenging times.

With your membership, you are instantly plugged into this rich and supportive environment. The Ladies Working Dog Group is more than just a group - it's a family. So, why wait? If you're a woman passionate about working dogs, come join us and be part of our evolution. You'll gain immediate access to our wealth of resources, including online training masterclasses, coaching recordings, events, our private podcast and so much more.

MEMBER SUCCESS STORIES

In this chapter, I've included success stories from our members. These aren't just random stories; they come straight from our Trustpilot page. Trustpilot is a well-known platform where users share their real experiences. By using these real-life reviews, we want to show you the true benefits our members have seen. If you're interested in more details, you can always visit our Trustpilot page to read more reviews from our community.

Debbie – Brilliant value and a genuine community
"The LWDG has given me so much confidence as a handler and owner. They have put the fun back into training and really helped us build a fantastic bond. The fabulous team and awesome members are always there to share their experiences and offer advice. There is so much great content, in many useful formats, that can be used out in the field or at home. Brilliant value for money and would recommend it to any female working dog owner, whatever their experience. It is a genuine community."

Luna - Fun, Helpful and Informative Group
"So happy I found this fun, inclusive group of women where experts generously share their knowledge, time and passion. I am a complete beginner and have learnt so much and feel a lot more confident with my dog training. It is a place where you are not made to feel silly for asking any questions you may have; everyone is so happy to help."

Jill - LDWG completely changed the way I train…
"LDWG completely changed the way I train my dog. Their support is invaluable to me, and I could not imagine my training life without them now. They have helped me get over some issues I've encountered in training and helped me build my confidence. There is so much advice offered both on the social media platform and in the masterclasses that are accessible as a member. I always look forward to the coaching and Q&A sessions."

Sue - Life changing

"If you're looking for a totally supportive, positive and super-helpful network then look no further, you're in the right place. Joining the LWDG has been one of the best things I've ever done. I've made some great friends and am constantly blown away by the depth of knowledge that is shared by the experts and in the masterclasses. Absolutely love this group."

Gill - A Fantastic Group

"What a fabulous group this is. The experts are truly great, giving up their valuable time to provide really helpful Masterclasses and other informative videos, chats and the like. Their knowledge, skill at imparting it and keenness to be so helpful is second to none. The icing on the cake is the wonderful Jo who brought her fabulous idea of a working dog group for ladies to fruition and who holds it all together so brilliantly. Thank you, ladies."

Paula - Fantastic Group!

"This is a great group to belong to and I am so glad that I found it. It is very active, well-managed and supportive, and has a fantastic array of training events and resources available to members. As a novice handler of my first working dog, I have found being part of a community of like-minded ladies hugely reassuring. It is amazing to know that there is always an expert on hand to answer any questions or to provide advice on any issues I may be having. I am thoroughly enjoying learning with my dog, and keeping up with how others, and their dogs, are getting on too!"

Nic - My Dogs Are Glad I'm A Member of LWDG!!
"This is an amazing group to be a member of. I have learnt so much and will continue to. A range of advice, coaching sessions, masterclasses and more are available, plus advice on any aspect of training and life with a working dog. So much knowledge among the group members and experts. Friendly and kind, always supportive of each other."

Alyson - Joining this group has made me think...
"Joining this group has made me think about every aspect of training my young gun dog, despite having trained dogs before. It is an exceptionally supportive informative platform... well done Jo and team... look forward to each week's sessions, be it videos, Hot Mess Handler sessions or podcasts."

HOW MEN CAN ENGAGE WITH THE LWDG

If you're a gentleman reading this chapter, we're glad you're interested. Whilst our community is female only, we still want to support you where we can. We invite you to listen to our LWDG Podcast 'Found It, Fetched It' to learn more about working dogs.

You're also welcome to enrol in our flagship course, "The Hot Mess Handler", accessible to both men and women. "The Hot Mess Handler" is your comprehensive guide to working with your dog. Even if you're very skilled, handling a working dog can sometimes be tricky. This course helps you with all the know-how and practical skills you need to work well with your dog. It is packed with easy-to-follow tips and advice, all aimed at solving the usual problems you might face with a working dog. It covers everything from how to make a strong connection with your dog to train the foundational cues, to understanding their behaviours and what they need. It can even help turn the most difficult situations into great chances to learn.

Ladies, if you're a member of our Society, you can access this amazing course for free. So, whether you're new to working with dogs or you're an expert, "The Hot Mess Handler" is a fantastic tool that can help you get even better. Together, we're making a difference in the world of working dogs for all.

THANK YOU

Writing *The Thoughtful Dog Trainer: Your Mindset Journey as a Working Dog Owner* has been an unforgettable experience, an adventure that would not have been possible without the contribution, support and influence of many individuals.

To my father, Ray Sheldon, who, without a doubt, has changed the lives of thousands of dog owners. I wish you were here to see the ripple effect of your wisdom. Even though you are no longer with us, your memory and your guidance continues to influence and inspire me and many more people that you never met but who thank you.

To my mother Linda, the unsung hero of my story. Whilst I often speak of Dad's influence, I never forget that you have been even more pivotal in me reaching my goals. Your words of encouragement have echoed throughout my life, and they have never been in vain. I hear every word.

To my loving husband Matthew. You have been there in times of success, cheering me on, and in times of struggle, sitting beside my hospital bed when fear felt like my only companion. Your steadfastness is the rock upon which I lean, and your love, my sustaining force. Every one of my achievements is also yours. I am incredibly grateful for you, my Mr. P.

To my beautiful children, Charlotte, Robert and Megan. Thank you for the smiles that fuel me, the fun that makes it all worth it and the chaos that propels me forward. Your support and love mean everything. My hope is that my life has shown you that no matter what the difficulties are, one can always persevere and overcome them. Also, to my daughters, you are fierce and fabulous proof-readers. Many mistakes were removed, and many paragraphs improved through your wonderful attention to detail. Thank you.

To the amazing LWDG Group Experts, Claire Denyer, Jemma Martin, Emma Stevens and Samantha Thorneycroft-Taylor. I am deeply grateful to you for standing by me through thick and thin. Your constant support and faith in me, and our work within the LWDG has been instrumental in its amazing success. You have consistently spurred me on, preventing me from losing faith in myself or in my mission. To all the other amazing experts and coaches, thank you for stepping forward to support me and the LWDG community. Each of you has made a permanent mark in helping our community.

To the vibrant community of the Ladies Working Dog Group - never forget that you can do this. Your shared experiences, both the struggles and victories, contribute to our collective success. Keep growing, keep sharing, and know that we are here for you.

To my beta readers, and to Authors & Co, you were invaluable in getting my book off my vision board and into reality. Without your support, I'm sure I would have given up and put this book on a shelf to die.

To Will Hetherington, thank you for providing a platform for me to share my interviews and connect with an audience that shares our passion for working dogs. The articles we have created together helped build my confidence that I could do this.

I am eternally grateful to each one of you. To all those mentioned and unmentioned, you have my heartfelt thanks.

REFERENCES

Canfield, J. (2005). *The Success Principles (TM)* - 10th Anniversary Edition: How to Get from Where You Are to Where You Want to Be. HarperCollins Leadership.

Castillo, B. (2008). *Self-Coaching 101*. Futures Unlimited Coaching.

Pavlov, I. P. (1927). *Conditioned reflexes: An investigation of the physiological activity of the cerebral cortex.* London: Oxford University Press.

Fisher, J. (2012). *Think dog.* Cassell Illustrated.

Middleton, A. (2022). *The Wall.* HarperCollins.

ABOUT THE AUTHOR

Joanne Perrott, the author and visionary behind *The Thoughtful Dog Trainer: Your Mindset Journey as a Working Dog Owner*, is a trailblazer in the world of dog training and women's development. As the founder of The Ladies Working Dog Group, a global membership community for women aspiring to train their dogs, Joanne has dedicated countless hours to helping her peers gain confidence and success in this challenging yet rewarding endeavour.

Certified as a Canfield Success Principles Trainer, Joanne brings her vast experience in personal development to her writing, underpinned by her academic understanding of human behaviour from her Certificate of Higher Education in Psychology from the University of South Wales. She offers her readers a unique and inspiring perspective on achieving personal dog training success, merging psychological principles with practical techniques. Joanne is also a respected contributor to the Gundog Journal, a publication recognised throughout the sport of gundog training. She has also been featured on BBC Radio and in magazines, including Gundog Journal and The Field Magazine.

Joanne resides in South Wales, UK, with her loving family. She shares her life with her supportive husband, Matthew, their three children, Charlotte, Robert and Megan, and their three dogs, two English Springer Spaniels and a feisty Cava Poo cross. Matthew's unwavering support during Joanne's brave fight against three brain tumours has been a testament to their enduring love and companionship. The courage and resilience displayed by Joanne throughout this difficult time serve as a testament to her strength and tenacity.

Joanne draws inspiration from influential authors such as Jack Canfield, Les Brown and Jim Rohn. Each has played a significant role in shaping her outlook on life, reinforcing her belief in her own capabilities and influencing the empowering narratives that she brings to her writing. The courage and passion encapsulated in her personal life and professional accomplishments make Joanne a source of inspiration, resonating deeply with her readers, making Joanne an influential voice in the realms of personal growth and dog training.

When Joanne isn't talking dogs, or helping the LWDG community to thrive, she can be found with her family and friends, learning to play the piano or in a sugar craft class!

---

instagram.com/JoannePerrott

Printed in Great Britain
by Amazon

38620676R00128